MW01710989

"WHEN I GROW TOO OLD TO LAUGH
Shoot me!"

"WHEN I GROW TOO OLD TO LAUGH
Shoot me!"

A Collection of Newfoundland Humour by
AL CLOUSTON

Manufactured in Canada by Webcom Limited

ISBN 0-9690904-5-5

Published 1986 by

Al Clouston Publications
P. O. Box 5922
St. John's, Nfld., A1C 5X4

No part of this book may be reproduced in any form without permission in writing from the publisher.

DEDICATION

My previous two books of Newfoundland humour were dedicated to the very ones who created it. Mainly the fisherman, the logger, the miner and the farmer. He was and still is the one who is the producer of this laughter, the ingredient which is needed in all areas of human life.

To him I dedicate once more my third edition of Newfoundland folklore humour.

FOREWORD

It has been said that our ability to laugh is the healthiest thing we can do. Al Clouston, over the years, has certainly demonstrated his unusual ability to tickle all our funny bones with his remarkable stories, jokes and Newfoundland humour. Certainly when we grow too old to laugh maybe shooting us is not the solution; the solution is to remember that unless we become as little children we cannot enter the Kingdom. Laughter is the key to the Kingdom and we should never lose the ability to laugh at ourselves and to laugh at life's cosmic humour. Laughing together creates a comradeship that is dear to all of us.

Al Clouston is a true Newfoundland hero. He has gone through many reincarnations and he handles everything he does with ease, efficiency, and always with good humour. It is wonderful to see him producing these books of humour. They are Al's contribution to the expanding culture of Newfoundland and of Canada.

I should mention that Pierre Berton on a series of national radio programs, has been discussing Canadians worthy of note calling them "Canadian Achievers," and he has singled out Al Clouston as one of them. For his success in compiling and publishing books and albums of Canadian humour that has so enriched our lives through the volumes of laughter he has created, Pierre has recently named Al as a great "Canadian Achiever."

I am sure that everybody who enjoys this book will feel better for taking the time to read it, and to remember some of the funny stories so that they can enrich the lives of their friends and neighbours.

As Newfoundlanders we admire Al Clouston a great deal. He is one of our Newfoundland folk heroes and may this book be tremendously successful. May Al continue to tickle our funny bones and add to the enjoyment that a good laugh brings anytime and anywhere.

G.W. Stirling
Publisher
The Newfoundland Herald

INTRODUCTION

Folklore humour is the type you can recognize as being original because, as one of my fans put it, you know no one stayed up half the night dreaming it up.

Folklore humour is generated in the rural areas of any country. Through my travels I have learned that it has the same flavour in one country as another. This is because people in rural areas live more closely together community wise and it is one of their pass-times, a form of entertainment or almost sport, to make humourous remarks about or poke fun at one another without risking resentment or antagonism.

Newfoundlanders have experienced this kind of humour for centuries. Living a way of life which was both tough and dangerous, they knew instictively that their labour had to be interspersed with a constant relief, and how better could they have it than by comic relief and seeing it in one another. I have experienced this drama myself by standing close by, where a dozen fellows have been working in stage putting away fish, and have heard this banter of conversation sprinkled with explosions of laughter.

While reading the stories in this book enjoy them by visualizing the action because most are true. A few are nonsense but remember that nonsense is the best entertainer.

Al Clouston

'TIS THIS WAY

For many years I have been listening to the humour of our island people and telling it to all I rub shoulders with each day all over the country. It is basic folklore humour and I give humorous addresses on the subject. Also I have been documenting it by writing books and recording it in voice.

It amazes me just how much humour and laughter have taken over in my life. I know to some people I don't sound sensible because in some way each topic I discuss is turned into humour at some point in the conversation. Very recently in a public place a lady came looking to see who and what was causing all the laughter. When she saw me she approached me and said "You should see a physhiatrist." Laughlingly I replied "I couldn't be that lucky because it is only sensible people who find it necessary to see a phychiatrist." She walked away, still convinced she was right.

The title of this book is nothing more than a fact of life. Let me tell you that if my friends heard "hello" from me when they telephone, they would get a shock. "Hello" on the telephone, in the tone most people say it, is such a cold greeting anyhow. My usual greeting is one of these in a voice well able to be heard. "Yes mam?", "Well, what now?", "Yes b'y", or "He's not here." Then they usually say "I'm looking for Al Clouston.", to which I reply, "You got um."

In my average walking day, I acknowledge many people whom probably I have never seen before. It is surprising how many people want to say hello to you and only need a little prompting. Try it. I know you will get a surprise also and you will feel better.

I tell my audience that I must have fun every day. One area which produces much fun is wrong numbers. Here is a sample. "Is Mabel there?", and I reply, "I wish she was. I'm here all alone." A voice says, "Is this the Mount Pearl Taxi?" This time I loudly say, "No." then in an invitingly soft voice I add, "but I'd love to come and pick you up." Then the lady caller says, "That might be nice, sir, but I think I'd better get the Taxi." Over and out, but not without a laugh from both of us.

I write a weekly column for the Newfoundland Herald and it has gotten me into many Newfoundland homes. Recently many letters have arrived at my door and these letters are so intimate that I feel I have many relatives. Last week I wrote and I quote, "It is just great to have heard from so many readers. Your comments about Uncle Al's column suggest that I am one of your family. You express yourselves as if you know me intimately. How nice it is that just by telling stories about ourselves we have all become related." Unquote.

Getting back to laughter, it has been said that laughter is the best medicine in the world. I have heard this rumoured for years, but more recently I'm reading it in fact. Dr. Charles Fry of Stanford University, California, prescribes fifteen minutes of good hard laughter for his worst arthritic patients, to reduce pain. Dr. Richard Johnson of the U.S. says this, "I believe that people who have a good sense of humour are likely to live longer, not coming down with so many probably stress related diseases." and he adds, "And that's probably why Santa Claus has lived so long. Ho-Ho-Ho."—Witness George Burns and Bob Hope. It is a medical fact that those who laugh the most live the longest, so I'm going for the hundred.

In April of this year I spoke at the Arthritis Bluebird Club. In their letter of thanks they told me about one of their members who telephoned the president and said that after laughing so much that evening she experienced the best night's sleep she had had for many months.

Who can match the smile of a baby, as the old song goes—SO LET A SMILE BE YOUR UMBRELLA FOR ANY RAINY DAY.

Al Clouston

Laughter

Laughter is precious. It can rescue us from an embarrassing situation. It can give us a fresh approach to a problem. It can help us keep a sense of proportion. Laughter offers physical benefits, too. It makes us breathe deeper, exercises the diaphragm and makes the wrinkles that are bound to appear in our faces pleasant ones. Laughter even makes friends – laugh and the world laughs with us. As the French say: "The most completely lost of all days is that on which one has not laughed!"

PROTESTANTS ARE HONEST?

Many years ago Father Coady in Tor's Cove purchased while in St. John's two bottles of rum. He placed them on the back seat of his car but when he went to take them out when he arrived back home there was only one bottle there. He exclaimed,

PETER'S FUNERAL

When Peter died, an old friend of Marie's and Peter's phoned me. It was the middle of February but I said to myself, "Even if I am caught down there the rest of the winter I'm going to Peter's funeral."

I arrived there nine o'clock the next morning. I went into the house and Mrs. Lee came from upstairs. Well, she got a real surprise and she came over to me, put her arms around me, laid her head on my shoulder and cried. I told her that we could do no more for Peter now and I had come just to spend the day with her.

We had breakfast and a man who seemed to be in charge of things came to me and rather secretly asked me if I was going to stay for the rosary to which I replied, "I came down for the funeral and I'm staying for everything that's goin'."

Well, we had the rosary and about 10 minutes later the same man announced, in a magnificent old Irish accent, "Anyone here now wants to have a loook (look) at this good man before we clouse 'um op?" Then when people had finished paying their last respects, the man in charge stood by the casket and said, "Well, good loook (luck) to ya now," and then he closed the casket. Let me hasten to say that there was no sacrilege in that pronouncement; it was a prayer and nothing else.

The casket was placed on a half-ton pickup and just then Mrs. Lee came out of the house. I asked her to get in the car with me, which she did. I was the first car to start and the pickup was directly behind me. At the time, I had a black Buick sedan and the thought struck me, if only Geoff Carnell would come along right now.

There were about 300 people at that funeral mass, all Catholics. But who was the chief mourner coming down the aisle, immediately behind the casket, with Mrs. Lee on his arm—if it wasn't meself. She was happy about it and so was I.

Some weeks later I was telling my barber Frank O'Toole, who was held office well up in the Knights of Columbus, all about the funeral and his comment was, "Yes, and you were the only black Protestant 'dere," and that was true.

ANOTHER WAKE

This is another story about a wake. Yes, a wake back in these times was equal to a wedding. (The fight was optional in some cases). In this small outport an old lady had died, we'll call her Aunt Mattie and the wake was in full swing.

The old house where she had lived was all lit up and the whole village turned out to pay their last respects to Aunt Mattie.

A big scoff was being prepared, etc. Soon old Aunt Mattie was laid out in the parlor in her best bib and tucker. Her coffin rested on a table covered by a cloth, candles burned at her head and feet.

Friends and relatives came and went and some came back again. Well into the night there was a lull in the number of visitors arriving. Those who were staying all night were gathered in the big kitchen and the corpse was left all alone in the parlor.

Suddenly someone smelled cloth burning. Aunt Sooze and a couple more women rushed in where the coffin was and found the table cloth all afire.

Well, quickly they douted the flames. What happened was a candle had burned down and caught the cloth afire that covered the table.

When all the fuss had subsided an old fellow in a pepper and salt cap sitting by the kitchen stove smoking away at his pipe made this comment, "puir auld Mattie if dey hadna discovered ut sa quick she'd a bin burned da det."

A LITTLE EAVESDROPPING CAN BE FUN

Today I'm going to confess to eavesdropping but not quite as serious as listening in on a political caucus which we heard all about recently.

What I'm talking about is when I see two old fellas yarnin' on the waterfront on Water Street. I get quite close to them to learn what they are talking about, and then at the right moment I'll chime in with something humorous. Then one of them turns to see who is butting in and when he sees me, he usually comes back with something much funnier than what I said. Then of course, I let go with one of my bellylaughs to be heard all over Water Street.

That is exactly what happened one day last year right by the Nonia store. At the time there was a lady coming towards me in the crosswalk there. She stepped up on the sidewalk and did not stop until she stood in front of me. She was much shorter than I, so she looked up at me and said "Mister, you laughs right from d'bottom of yer stomach don't ya?" That set me right off on a real laughing jag. 'Tis good fer what ails ya.

Another time I was listening to two other fellas who were from over 'ome. They were right on the corner of Water Street and Adelaide Street. What they were discussing was the fact that the provincial government had brought a huge statue of the Portuguese explorer and navigator, Corte-Real, and placed that statue away in the country in front of the Confederation Building.

Well they were not at all in agreement with putting Corte-Real in there and eventually one of them said, "Dat Joey Smallwood, he's got nar bit sinse t'all. 'Eh sends over to Portugal an' gits Corte-Real and puts 'n in on a farm. Sher 'eh wouldn't a farmer eh wuz a navigator. Eh should be down 'ere 'long we, down be d' landwash."

THE PRICE OF HEAVEN

Some people have a motive when they give to their church or some philanthropic cause. They are building up a credit in their minds in the hope of a reward. The following story tells us about a man who had that kind of thinking.

A certain man was the most generous giver in the congregation. One day the pastor was remarking to him what a grand thing he was doing being such a support to the church. The man responded by saying he felt the same way. He added that he thought that it pleased the Lord and it would be remembered when he passed on to that other world.

He next said to the pastor that he knew how much he had given and wondered how much more he would have to give to bring about the reward he had in mind. The pastor was not prepared to give a reply on the spur of the moment but he would think about it and try to get the answer for his parishoner.

A few weeks passed and when they met again the pastor told his parishoner that the amount would be twenty-five thousand dollars. Then pastor added, "One more thing. Be ready next Saturday."

DODGIN THE FOREMAN

In a large garment producing establishment a new foreman had been hired in an effort to increase efficiency.

His name was Dodgin.

On his first inspection tour he came upon a machine which was idle and the operator was partly out of sight in the corner. The foreman said to him, "I'm Dodgin, the new foreman." The employee replied, "So am I, come and sit down and we'll have a chat."

A CHOICE—COW OR TOURIST

In his travels a tourist came to a ferry crossing where a farmer acted as the ferryman for the odd traveller. It was a very stormy day and the farmer was getting ready to make a crossing just when the tourist arrived.

The farmer agreed to take the tourist across but he would have to wait until he ferried his cow over first.

The farmer set out with his cow and in an hour or so returned for the tourist. They were about half way across when the tourist asked, "How come you made me wait until you took your cow over–" The farmer replied, "Well, now 'tis this way. The cow is the most valuable cow I have. I feared the wind would increase and the boat might upset on the second trip."

WHAT DIFFERENCE?

From a reader: While travelling to the Burin Peninsula a few years ago, we had to go by way of the Conception Bay Highway to pick up an elderly couple. A short while before this, the seat-belt law had come into effect.

The cab driver put the lady in the front between him and her husband. He next fastened her seatbelt. The old gentleman, however, had considerable difficulty. He fumbled about for three or four minutes searching for one end of the seatbelt and finally gave up and said, "Dat's alright b'y, I'll git 'er done up when we stops in Marystown."

ABOUT WATERBEDS

I told the gathering that, during June, I was standing in line on Friday afternoon at the bank. I spoke to a number of people whom I knew in the lineup and then turned my attention to the man immediately behind me. He was a pleasant chap and he told me he knew who I was and then put this question to me in a very Irish accent: "Skipper, why did d'man have to t'row away his waterbed?"

I said, "You tell me."

"Because his wife's side froze over."

TWO WHEELS

Dave Buckingham told me a true story about when he was attending the Memorial University.

He told me that in the class were two or three Roman Catholic sisters. They were easily distinguishable by their traditional long black dresses and shawls and other pieces of the habit.

In the middle of the semester an edict had been published by the Pope that allowed the sisters to discard their traditional dress and wear skirts and blouses with kerchiefs on their heads. The sisters in the class immediately adopted the new dress and some in the class did not recognize those new students.

One afternoon a male friend of Dave's was glancing around the room and as he looked backwards he recognized Sister Mary Acquin for the first time. He kept looking back at her and each time looked down at her legs. Sister caught him a couple of times when he looked at her and when she could stand it no longer she burst forth with a real class stopper, including the lecturing professor, and this is what she said, "WHAT DID YOU THINK I HAD UNDER THEM LONG DRESSES—TWO WHEELS?"

ALL HE GOT WAS NAR CHRISTMAS!

Some years ago in the month of January I met a friend on Water Street who had spent Christmas on the Burin Peninsula.

He said that one afternoon he was in a shop and was listening to two old fellas yarnin'.

Suddenly one said, "Look at 'n, dere's Joe comin' dere. Eh's a fullish feller, went h'off an' joined Jehovers Witness. Wonder what eh got outa dat."

The other replied, "I allow ol' man all eh got outa dat, wuz nar Christmas!"

MY HUSBAND'S SEAT

Visiting St. John's from a small outport, a man decided to attend a play at the Arts and Culture Center. On the night in question, he noticed a vacant seat much closer to the stage, so he approached the woman sitting next to it and asked if the seat was taken.

"No," she replied, "it was my husbands, but he died and I still have the ticket."

"Why didn't you give it to a relative or a friend?" She was asked.

"I couldn't," she answered, "they're all at his funeral."

MY WIFE MILDRED

"I don't know what I'm going to do about my wife Mildred," the Newfoundland businessman complained to his friend, "she keeps asking me for money. The day before yesterday she wanted $100, yesterday $75, and this morning, $60."

"What does she do with all that money?" The friend asked.

"I don't know," said the husband, "I've never given her any."

OLD-TIME FUNERALS IN NEWFOUNDLAND

It was no surprise to the bereaved when things got going. While some got a big scoff on, others were coming with things they had baked. The toime was seldom a cost upon the house. Inevitably, an accordion appeared, and how can feet lay flat on the floor when the owner hears the inviting music of the accordion. Sure it goes without saying a dance or two was held in the kitchen.

Practical jokes were not excluded either. The young fellows usually took part in this activity. A story I heard 20 years ago was that about three in the morning two young men found a couple of pulleys and rope. They secured the rope to the door, passed it through the pulleys and then secured the rope to the shoulders of the corpse. It was arranged that when anyone opened the door the corpse would sit upright. The man they most wanted to frighten was told to go in and of course it had the expected effect. He came out looking for the two young fellows but they had disappeared and did not show themselves 'till the next day.

A clergyman friend of mine died here in the city. It was the week between Christmas and New Year's. I went dutifully to see his wife at Barrett's Funeral Home. When I entered the room, she came right over to me and when we had talked for a minute, she then surprised me by introducing me to all the other people in the room. Then she hinted that maybe I would tell the gathering a couple of my stories. The people seemed to forget the reason for their being there and laughed without any trouble. The circumstances in that room were the same after I told these stories as before, but the gloom was gone. Maybe the widow wanted to experience something of her earlier life in a small outpot community.

A SURPRISING APPETITE!

A young Newfoundlander went to Toronto to find himself a job. He found himself a job but he was also successful in finding himself a Torontonian for a girlfriend. Wishing to impress this lady he asked her to one of the better eating places for dinner.

The waitress approached their table and asked them if they were ready to order. The girlfriend was more than ready for she ordered as follows:

A double shrimp cocktail

Pea soup

A steak

Broccoli

Roast potato

Buttered carrots

Cauliflower

Baked alaska

Fruit cocktail.

Then she turned to the boyfriend and said "I wonder what I'll have to drink?" To which our Newfoundlander replied, "HOW ABOUT ONE OF THE GREAT LAKES?"

THE ESSENCE OF CONTRARINESS

A Newfoundland couple had been married for many years. The wife was very patient because she had put up with a lot of contrariness from her husband. The incident which went a bit too far was when he came to breakfast one morning and she said,

Wife: What are ya goin' to 'ave fer yer brakfass?

Husband: Two h'eggs.

Wife: How do ya want 'em?

Husband: One boiled an' one fried.

She did as he requested and put the eggs on the table in front of him. When he scowled and frowned at the same time she said,

Wife: What's wrong now?

Husband: Ya boiled d' wrong one.

A NEWFOUNDLAND SPINSTER WHO LIVED ALONE

A Newfoundlander spinster who lived alone, got the urge for a rabbit pie one day, so she hurried off to the corner grocery store to buy one for her evening meal.

When she got there she was disappointed to see the few remaining rabbits were much too large for her needs.

"Oh my sar," she moaned, "is dere any way I can git just a half one?"

The grocer leaned across the counter, looked down at the little old lady and said with a straight face. "I'm sorry mam, but we don't split hares."

On holiday in Toronto, a young Corner Brook girl wandered into a boutique and looked over the display of sweaters. As she removed one from the rack, a saleslady walked over.

"Isn't $120 a lot for a sweater?" The Newfoundlander asked.

"Not at all," replied the saleslady, "it's pure wool, shorn from a special breed of sheep who live in the most inaccessible region of the Himalayan mountains; it's truly a beautiful yarn."

"It sure is," said the Corner Brooker, "and you tell it so well."

THE WRONG BATH

Before Confederation with Canada, ordering from Eaton's and Simpsons was very popular all over the island. Many families bought all their wearing apparel from H'Eaton's and many other items as well.

One story I was told was about a man on Bell Island who ordered all his bathroom fixtures from H'Eatons. The wash basin he ordered was the one he had chosen from the catalogue and so was the toilet, but the bath was definitely not from the catalogue. The clerk in the ordering office argued that it had to be the one he ordered because it matched the basin and toilet.

After awhile the clerk told him to go to the office upstairs and tell them about it. Upstairs, the manager and two office people got involved and eventually the manager suggested they get the catalogue and check it out. But just then, the catalogue could not be found. In exasperation the manager said, "well, please tell us what the difference is between the one you ordered and the one that came for you." So the Bell H'Islander replied "Well, ol' man, I'll tell eh now. D'bat' I saw in d'catalogue an' h'ardered, 'ad a woman in it."

A chap from Port-de-Grave was asked "So youse builllding a new 'ouse! 'ows it comin?"

"First rate. I've got the roof and mortgage on, and I spects to have the furnace and sherriff in before fall."

THERE HAS TO BE A FIRST TIME

Some very funny stories have been sent to me recently, and I am most grateful to those people who have taken time out to write these stories.

The following story ends in disaster. Truthfully, I could barely get the story ready for print due to my laughing. I have said this before, try and imagine the scene and the participants as you read.

I am going to relate the story just as I received it.

In the outports you had to do it all by yourself and also with many other things it included butchering. So young fellows attended the butchering of cattle with the fathers, uncles or neighbours. How else were they to learn, for one day they themselves would be the butcher, and woe betide the fellow who was squeamish. Why? He was sissy right then and there. To be labeled a sissy was something no young guy could stand.

In a certain community two older fellows were going to butcher a bull. So they took along their two teenage boys to help and observe how it was done. (These two weren't the sissy type by any means.)

So they rounded up the bull and tied it to an old rotten fish flake near the landwash. After throwing it an armful of hay to keep the bull quiet, the two elders went off for a cuppa tea before doing the job. They left the young fellas with the bull.

Now when the mind is idle the devil makes you do it—so these two began to get thoughts about doing the job by themselves. They argued as to who would strike the first blow. They had to start sometime so now was as good as any.

Bye and bye one fellow decided it would be him. They did not take into account their puny strength in swinging the maul. So picking up the maul this fellow swung it aiming for the bull's forehead. Just as he did, the bull whose head was down getting another mouthful of hay, rose his head and the blow took it right in the mouth. Well all hell broke loose. When the two old guys came back the bull was gone—the flake was gone—the two young boys were gone. Only the maul lay on the ground.

Well I'd better leave the rest to the reader's imagination.

Note from Uncle Al:

What a catastrophy. No steaks for supper!

EQUAL PAY FOR EQUAL WORK

It is quite evident that parity was not a word that existed in Bible imes.

At St. Pius X, Father Ficher was reading the gospel one Sunday a few years back and he read the parable which had to do with the orchard owner who paid the same wages for one hour's work as he did for eight hours.

When mass was over and the people were leaving the church a remark overheard by a close friend of the priest was, "yes," said an older parishoner, "it was alright for that orchard owner but he didn't have Fraser March to deal with."

SCHOOL DAYS

Visits to school by the Public Health Nurse goes back a long way. I remember when the nurse visited the old Methodist College on Long's Hill. (Some h'old isn't oi.)

Well, they had the same visits in the outport schools. On one occasion the nurse gave a child a form which was filled out, telling the parent the condition of the health of her offspring.

On reading this form, the parent became quite upsot. To put it mildly, she was right affronted. She summoned her child to the kitchen and asked, "Sarah, what's h'adenoids?"

Sarah replied, "Shur you knows mom, t'ings in yer 'ead what 'as to come out."

The mother turned on Sarah and said, "Look 'ere, oi fine toot's yer 'ead wit' d'comb h'every night and nar h'adenoid can oi find!"

CLOSE TO HEAVEN BY CAR

A typical example of folklore humour is the following story. I was requested in May this year to give an entertainment at Hr. Breton which is on the Sou'wess coast of Newfoundland.

The lady I stayed with, Rosie Strickland, told me about an older man who bought a car. He had never had a licence to drive a car before this, and people were rather reluctant to ride with him.

Eventually, a friend who was feeling sorry for the new driver, decided to accompany him on one occasion, when the friend was asked whether or not he was nervous he replied, "Well, I tell ya now. When he got her up to 50, I was singing 'ABIDE WITH ME'. When he got her up to 70 I sang 'NEARER MY GOD TO THEE' and when he got her up to 90 I sang, 'LORD I'M COMING HOME'.

WIFE AN ANGEL, DEAD OR ALIVE

Two men who had been bossom pals in their younger days, happened to meet after considerable years had elapsed.

They were comparing notes on their fortunes to date and eventually got around to discussing their families. One made several comments about his wife and finished by saying, "To tell you the truth my wife is an angel." Then the other exclaimed "B'y yer some lucky, my wife is still alive."

RHODES SCHOLAR

The local chairman of the political party was introducing the new candidate for the district and he was giving him quite a build-up.

He talked about his family background. What a great churchman he was and all the local committees he had headed up for local improvement. He was about to bring his remarks to a close when he suddenly remembered something and concluded with, "oh yes, and something else—our new candidate is a Rhodes Scholar."

At this remark, a fellow in the back of the hall stood up quickly and yelled, "Well, Mr. Chairman zir, d'lass ting ya said is d'feller we needs down 'ere. A feller what knows all about d'roads."

WHAT KIND OF DANCING

I have not participated too much in the rock-and-roll dancing of this modern day and when watching it a few times on T.V. I have wondered at the sanity of the performers.

On one occasion here locally an uncle and his nephew were on the side lines watching some of the antics of the people on the dance floor doing their version of rock-and-roll.

The nephew turned to the uncle and remarked, "I betcha Uncle you never saw dancing like that back in your day, hey Uncle?" The reply was, "yes b'y, I did once, when the place was raided."

EULOGY AND CORPSE DIDN'T MATCH

In a Catholic community in Newfoundland the priest was giving a eulogy to a deceased husband during the funeral mass. He kept making complimentary remarks about the man in the coffin. His praise for the deceased was so high that the widow was very doubtful whether or not it was about her dead husband that the priest was making his remarks. The man she knew and lived with was not that gentle and kind. So when the priest was finished the eulogy and sat down, she poked her daughter with her elbow and said.

SHE WAS "SOME UPSOT"

Visiting the motor vehicle registration office last year a gentleman from Brigus approached me and said that he is often asked to entertain at church functions and various socials as I am doing all through the year. On a number of occasions people have said to me, "Al, the people in the outports must be displeased with you because you are always imitating them, using their vernacular when telling your stories."

I reply, "Yes I think they must be very put out with me because I am invited by all these people you are talking about to entertain them with the very humour which they created. Yes, I think they must be real put out with me when they ask me to come and spend a few days with them."

Anyway, Mr. Jerrett of Brigus told me a very funny story that day. A man down the shore a piece from him has a setter dog. It is his habit to let the dog run loose for an hour each morning and then tie him up for the rest of the day.

One morning he left the kitchen to go and bar up the dog but only got to the back door, where he was stopped by a woman standing on the bridge. She was some h'ugly, she was in a passion and burst forth with, "Do you know dat your dog come down to my 'en 'ouse dis marning an' h'eat two me h'aggs and two me chicken?"

The owner of the dog hesitated in reply and then said "Well maid if 'e did 'e 'ad a better brakfass den I 'ad."

A POOR PLACE TO BE GOIN'

This happened over in Nar-Wes' Brook. What Nar-Wes' Brook I don't know. (Cuz there must be forty-eleven in Newfoundland.)

Fauder and mudder were having quite a tiff this morning. All he knew dat mudder was waitin' fer d'taxi and she would give him no satisfaction as where she was off to.

When the taxi arrived and she was going out through the hallway he yelled, "where's ya goin' mudder, where's ya goin'?" He got no answer. Just as she got in the taxi he yelled again, "Where's ya goin' mudder, where's ya goin'?" Still no answer.

When she was settled in the seat in the taxi she rolled down the window and shouted, "I'm goin' to 'ell." And he yelled back, "Yes, and if I 'ad d'passage money oi'd go dere too."

IT IS A CERTAINTY

A retail merchant on Water Street was sympathizing with the widow of a long time customer. She listened to all he had to say and then her only remark was, "Ah b'y, we all got to die. His turn came and he took it on."

THEM MAINLANDERS

In my travels to certain parts of mainland Canada I have come across a number of Newfoundlanders who disclaimed that they hailed from our island—a queer breed, eh? Then there are a few of us who want to disown certain Newfoundlanders just because we do not like them.

In the following I am quoting from a letter I received a couple of months ago from a mainlander who is a friend of Newfoundlanders. I have substituted fictitious names, of course.

Quote: "When I lived in Saint John, New Brunswick, there was a Newfoundlander across the street from me, Bill Brown and his wife Caroline, a registered nurse. Bill was a pretty come-day/go-day sort of fella, but Caroline had a strong tendency to put on the dog, quite unusual for a Newfoundlander. One evening, I was standing in front of my next door neighbour's house, talking to his wife and Caroline came across the street and joined us. While we stood there chatting, my neighbour arrived home, and, walking up to Caroline, said, 'Shake hands Caroline.'

"Caroline looked puzzled but nevertheless shook hands. 'That hand,' said my neighbour, 'just shook hands with Harry Hibbs!'

" 'Harry Hibbs?' said Caroline, 'Harry Hibbs? I don't know anything about anybody named Harry Hibbs.' Pause . . . 'Besides, I don't like that kind of music anyway.'"

THAT'S NOT WHAT MUDDER TOLD HIM

I am receiving a lot of help from readers who send in their humourous stories to me. This story comes from Sin Jan's, and of course, it is about a townie.

An Irish fella named Murphy worked in a garage in Sin Jan's and was an awful boozer. He took a job as third engineer on a Clarenville vessel running to the West Indies.

The trip south took 10 days and there wasn't a drop of spirits on board. On arrival at Barbados he was in heaven, what with good rum (as if any of it is good) at 90 cents a bottle.

The third day on our way home he appeared in the messroom looking pretty shaky and his first words were, "Me mudder told me to go away to sea on a ship to get clear of d'likker and I runned right into it."

THEY GOT THEIR JUST DESSERTS

Many times I have been asked when did I start to have fun telling stories and turning my experiences into fun. My reply is always that I don't remember when I didn't.

I can go back to my courting days when I was about twenty. We were a foursome and many times we went to Donovan's (Jack Robinson's), Brenicks at Forest Pond or Mrs. Berg's at Chamberlains. The meals at all these places were as good as you'd wish to find.

On one occasion we ordered a meal for four at a catering house at Holyrood. The hostess there was a very motherly woman and always gave us a grand welcome. One time however, the welcome was as warm as ever but the dinner was not as good as ever. It was not up to snuff as we used to say.

The chicken must have been an old cock of uncertain age. Not like the half chicken I had recently, which must have had a weight problem. The Holyrood chicken I refer to was some tough and we had to leave most of it.

It was the dessert that gave us the fun. It was chocolate pudding far from being edible. It stuck solidly to the roof of your mouth, mastication was not possible and the pallet refused to accept it. An egg timer must have been used for the cooking period. I said to the other three, "Well, I know I have to get clear of mine," then I took two serviettes and wrapped up my pudding in them and put it in my coat pocket. Just then herself walked in and said in surprise and disappointment, "Oh my, only one of you ate my pudding!" At that I stood up and lost my balance on the side where the pudding was in my coat pocket. My friends got the inference but I made a quick exit leaving them to parry the hostess's questions and my male partner to pay the bill.

GETTING YOUR OWN BACK

I have known individuals who, like Susie in our following story, had the courage to speak up and give the same as they received. As a matter of fact, I like 'em.

A clergyman's wife had employed a young lady, by the name of Susie, to come and help her with the domestic chores. One Sunday night Susie arrived in church late, due to her having to finish work in the rectory.

The next morning the reverend's wife asked Susie how she had enjoyed her husband's sermon. Susie replied, "I didn't hear much of it m'am cuz I came in on the tail end of it."

Her employer thought that she should try and improve her helper's English so she said, "Susie, never say 'tail end', you must always say conclusion."

A few days later Susie was getting breakfast and happened to look out the window and saw a dog running down the street with a tin can tied to its tail. This was her chance, so she called excitedly to the lady of the house and said, "M'am, m'am, come, come and see the little dog running down the road with a tin tied onto his conclusion!"

HAULING SWOILES

Two "Greenpeacers" were listening to two oldtimers in St. Anthony discussing "swoilers." Of course, they knew that many Newfoundlanders referred to seals as swoiles.

Thinking to have some fun one of these Greenpeacers said to them, "How do you spell swoiles?"

One of the oldtimers replied quickly, "We don't spell 'em we hawls 'em."

SHORT SERMONS

The preacher was very clever and impressive when giving forth during his sermons. One of his delights was to give verbal illustrations to highlight various points of his sermon.

On one occasion, he was telling his congregation how God was very evident in nature and could be seen in the forest, in the garden and even in the lawn, at that point he burst out with "Yes, why every blade of grass is a sermon!" Soon, the sermon was over.

The next day, the preacher was cutting his lawn when one of the older members of the parish was passing and he casually remarked, "Reverend, you're cutting your sermons short today."

PERCENTAGES

A Roman Catholic sister who was travelling all alone, found herself on an airliner seated directly in front of three protestant clergymen. She could overhear the conversation of the three which was mostly about the Roman Catholic denomination. Eventually one of the clergymen said, "I wished I lived in Canada. There are only 15% Catholics there. The next clergyman said he wished he lived in the United States, there are only 10% Catholics there. The third clergyman said, "You should live where I live, there's only 5% Catholics there."

Well the poor Catholic sister could take it no longer, so she turned around to them and said,

KNOW-IT-ALL

A friend of mine from Port-de-Grave told me of visits he made every month or so to see his aunt and uncle. It was usually a very pleasant visit.

One Saturday morning however he went to see them and after ten or fifteen minutes he realized that the atmosphere was not quite normal. Neither his uncle nor his aunt were in a very good mood. Apparently they had had a falling out over something.

My friend did not feel very comfortable but something happened to save the day. Someone knocked on the back door and Aunt Mary went out herself to see who it was. After a short conversation with someone we heard her ask a gentleman to come in. She didn't want to but it was the courteous thing to do.

He turned out to be a salesman who was marketing encyclopedias. He had a very good sales pitch but he saw that he was getting nowhere with a sale. Eventually he took a new line and he said, "Look, I am sure you two people have grandchildren, nephews and nieces and when they visit I am sure that they have questions and any which you do not have the answer for, you would surely find the answer in this encyclopedia." That was the opening Uncle Tom needed because he came to life and said, "me zon youm in d'wrong 'ouse, CUZ H'AUNT MARY 'ERE KNOWS H'EVERYTHING."

A LONG DAY'S NIGHT

For years a man had taken time out to go on a booze for himself for a month or so. As he got older he found he wanted to linger a little longer with the stuff and a month became two months before he would sober up.

On one of these longer trips he was sitting outside on the back of his house one morning. It was a beautiful sunny day but our friend couldn't determine what time of day it was. You have heard the remark, "He was so drunk for so long he didn't know night from day." Well this is where he was.

On this particular day he felt there was someone sitting near him and slowly raising his hand and glancing skywards and with a very thick tongue, said,

WHAT'S THE SECRET? SHUT YER MOUT'!

Through the last 20 years I have managed to keep my weight within range. In other words, the range from 158 pounds to 162 pounds. Many people mention this fact to me and say, "Al, you seem to keep your weight down."

I reply, "Yes, I have a secret."

They ask, "What's the secret?"

"Shut yer mout'!"

I contend that the first helping is for support, you know, it gives you the nourishment you need to keep you going. But the second helping is just luxury and usually you give in and say yes because you like the taste of it. Well that is where you get in trouble. Because once the taste experience is over and that second helping slips down the gullet you've had it. Then the second helping shows on yer—well wherever you show weight most. So take my advice and "Shut yer mout'." Be a weight watcher by watching the food go by.

POOR FISH

The following story is one I read recently and it is also about shutting your mouth. But it is a different kind of shutting your mouth because it carries with it some good advice. It is humorous but also has good philosophy on getting along together.

A man was passing a fishmonger's window and, looking in, he saw on display a large beautiful-looking salmon. There were two labels on it. The first gave the price, the other said dolefully, "If I had only kept my mouth shut!"

That night, the man mentioned it to his wife. She smiled. Then, more seriously, she said, "You know, it's a bit like us. How often one of us says a bit more than we meant, the thing develops into an argument, and we end up thinking, 'If only I'd kept my mouth shut!' . . ."

Her husband saw what she meant. Together they talked about it and they decided, from then on, if either was in danger of going a bit too far, the other would say two words as a kind of a secret warning: "Poor fish." Two words that bring back the memory of what happened to the salmon.

"If only I'd kept my mouth shut. . ." Good advice—and, unlike salmon fishing, there's no closed season.

THE PROPER PLACE FOR A FIGHT

A peculiarity noted in some areas of Newfoundland was what people would say about a wedding: "B'y it was a great weddin'. It ended up in a fight."

Well, I was at one of these weddin's 40 years ago. The bride was 19 and the bridegroom was 60. The first unusual thing to happen was that we were all in our places in the church on time. The bridegroom was there too. But, no sign of the bride. She showed up though, one hour late. Talk about being stood up at the altar, we thought it was going to happen this time.

This wedding took place some miles from St. John's. The bride was a young lady who was employed by a number of us fullish city fellas to work in our homes, on different days of the week. When the wedding came along she was kind enough to invite us all, and we went, about 20 of us I would say.

We did not know it but we were in for a treat. It was an excellent cold supper with delicious sweets—all cooked and made ready by herself.

The festivities went off in fine style, as we used to say when we assessed any social event after the fact.

But after midnight a fight broke out right after one of the dances. It was brought on by an act of chivalry over one of the local beauties. And what better reason could there be for a fight? The two contestants were about evenly matched. However, my brother mistaking himself for the bouncer, since he was a very strong fellow, and not wishing to see a pleasant evening end up in a brawl, decided he should do something about it. He got mixed up in the melee and came out of it with his arms locked around one contestant, lifted him completely off the floor, wound his way through the open doors onto the veranda and dropped him to the ground, a distance of about three feet. He re-entered the dance hall expecting to eliminate the other assailant in the same manner. But what a surprise! By the time he returned there were five different fights in progress all over the dance floor. Nobody was going to spoil the fun of this weddin'. They got their chance and took it. PROPER TING!

ABOUT MOOSE HUNTING

The best moose story I have told in the last two years was enjoyed most by moose hunters.

The drawing for moose licences became a lot of bother for the Wildlife Department and it did away with the whole system. It decided that everyone who applied for a moose licence would get one. But there were two stipulations: you were allowed one shot and it had to be at night.

One smart fellow got his licence and proceeded to do his hunting. He attached a flashlight to the barrel of his rifle and set off for the moose country. He was hunting for about two hours when the beam from the flashlight picked up a moose. He took aim and fired and hit the moose in the hoof. Well that wasn't too good so he took another shot and hit the moose through one of its ears. Dead moose.

He was just about to dress the moose when the Wildlife warden came along and examined the moose. He stood up and accused the man of taking two shots.

Hunter: "Naw b'y, naw, only one shot."

Warden: "Look here, this moose has the works of two shots."

Hunter: "Naw b'y, naw. Only one shot. I'll tell ya what happened. I held up the rifle with the flash light on it and the light from the flashlight got in the moose's eyes and when the moose held up his hoof to shade his eyes that's when I fired."

ONE ON THE MAINLANDERS

A visiting clergyman from the mainland told the following story at a meeting in the parish hall. I liked him for it because at last I had met a mainlander who was laughing at himself—the mainlander—something we Newfoundlanders do best of all.

He told the story about a certain section of Toronto where living was pretty rough. The owner of the beer parlour couldn't find a bouncer strong enough to keep order in the establishment. He resorted to getting a gorilla and trained him to remove the rowdies out onto the sidewalk. He chained the gorilla to a strong pillar in the corner and when a fight broke out he would let the gorilla go and peace was restored in short order.

One night a Newfoundlander came to the beer parlour and got involved in a fight. In about five minutes he knocked out four or five patrons. The gorilla was set loose and the Newfoundlander and the gorilla went through the door struggling, door shut. In about two minutes the door opened and the Newfoundlander came back in, shut the door, dusted himself off and then said loudly:

"DAT'S D'TROUBLE WIT' DEM MAINLANDERS. YA PUTS A FUR COAT ON 'EM AN' DEY T'INKS DEY OWNS D'WORLD."

HARD TIMES FOR SURE

I have often remarked how humorous stories evolve in Newfoundland.

A number of people may be sitting in the kitchen just yarnin', gathered on the wharf or just happen to meet in the general store, and what started out with a small conversation turns into a story telling session. They may be fabricated, fantastic and preposterous, but so what, everyone had a good laugh. To prove this, here's what I received in the mail.

A fellow from Corner Brook who worked on the C.B.C. Tower in Port Aux Basques, said they were sitting in a tavern chewing the fat and havin' a mug-o-beer. An old fellow came in and sat down with them and started talking about times gone by and the usual funny stories started.

The old fellow said that one time he visited a nearby community and saw a crowd of fellas on the wharf all bunched together, so he went down to where they were at to see what was goin' on. This is what followed. They were tying rocks on an old Waterloo stove for to sink it.

He continued and said that when he was a boy times were very hard in their community, so hard in fact that a man who lived nearby with seven sons said, when the boys got up in the mornin' he had to bar the old woman in the room so they wouldn't eat her.

HE COULDN'T RESIST

Dermot Duggan, my artist, told me about one day in school the Christian Brother was giving a lesson in grammar and what paraphrasing was all about.

He wrote on the black-board certain sentences which were for class discussion, and each student was to make a short statement when he was called upon.

The sentence about which Derm was called upon to make his statement was 'He was bent on seeing her.' His short statement was, 'The sight of her doubled him up.' and then the brother doubled Derm up.

A SEEK HOARSE, BUT HE DIED

I visited Renews on the Southern Shore to entertain at a Kinsmen meeting. After the meeting, a man came along and told me this story.

"Mr. Clusson, a man up d'shore had a hoarse an' he was seek." He met his friend and he said:

He went home and gave 'um da turpentine an' den he met his friend again.

"How did ya yet on wid d'hoarse? Did ya give 'um d'turpentine?"

"Yes I did."

"What happened?"

TRIP TO BAY D'ESPOIR

About 1961, I made a visit to the Sou'west coast. Wishing to go to Bay d'Espoir, a friend and I travelled to Bay L'Argent, Fortune Bay, having in mind to join the Government coastal boat, the *M.V. Bonavista*, on Saturday afternoon. When we arrived there, we were informed that the boat would not be there until six o'clock tomorrow morning. Well, it meant an overnight stay in Bay L'Argent and where were we going to sleep, surely not the car? I said this out loud and a C.N. employee suggested Mrs. Pardy's for she had a boarding house. I went up to Mrs. Pardy's and this is the following conversation:

Al: "Mrs. Pardy, do you have a bed for my friend and me, until the *Bonavista* gets in tomorrow morning?"

Mrs. Pardy: "Nar bed leaved now, zir. Dem all give up to salesmen and fellas like youse waitin' fer the Bonivess."

Al: "Well, what will we do now?"

Mrs. Pardy: "Go up to Banfields and wait there and we'll send a taxi there to let yees know when the Bonivess gets in."

Al: "Nothing cookin'. That boat'll come in, the captain will drop his freight and away to go. He won't wait for us."

My Friend: "Yer right, Al. Captain Penney is aboard dat Bonivess and he'll wait fer nobody. Last year down in St. Anthony he wouldn't wait half an hour fer me to finish a job. He said he wouldn't wait fer his own mother."

Mrs. Pardy: "Too bad 'bout'n! His mudder 'ad to wait nine mont's on ee."

HE ASKED ONE QUESTION TOO MANY

It was customary in the parish for the new pastor to visit his parishioners at their homes. Sometimes the head of the house was not at home and the pastor would visit him on the job.

When visiting one of the homes, he was told by the wife that her husband was down in the stage putting away fish. The pastor proceeded to the stage and was greeted kindly by a man who was much older than himself.

The conversation eventually got around to how long the family had been in this community.

Pastor: "I suppose your ancestors came here a long time ago."

Parishioner: "Yes zir, a long time. Yes dat's tru, a long time."

Pastor: "You can remember your grandfather?"

Parishioner: "Yes zir. I minds eh alright. Yes zir, I minds'n."

Pastor: "How about your great grandfather, do you remember him?"

Parishioner: "No zir, Don't mind eh. Cartny eh wuz deed when I come, No zir, don't mind'n."

"I suppose you could trace your ancestors back to Noah and the Ark?"

Parishioner: "No Zir, No zir, me fauder build eh's own skeef."

LONELY AND MISERABLE

A friend of mine who is a widow told me that her husband had said to her on one occasion, "It is better to be lonely than miserable." Talking to a bachelor in the post office one day I related this to him. His reply was, "Do you know what I say—'tis better to be miserable alone."

LORD REST EE'S SOUL

Labrador Fishery." Codfish were in abundance there and fishing crews from Conception Bay and Trinity Bay and other parts would go to Labrador fishing.

They would be gone all summer and very little news was received from them until they returned in the fall.

When serious accidents befell them, then of course, they went out of their way to get the news back home. On one occasion a man was drowned and, of course, the local minister received the message and it was part of his vocation to go and inform the family.

When he arrived at the home of the deceased the wife was dishing up large platefuls of fish and brewis. She sat down and started to eat and the minister was doing his best to break the news gently. Eventually he got to the point and advised that her husband was drowned.

She put down her fork, looked up and said, "Poor Gorge, ee's gone, ee's gone. Lord rest ee's soul. 'Old on till I gets me fish and brewis below, DEN YOU'LL HEAR D'SCREECHES."

WHAT DID OLD MACDONALD HAVE?

Three men answered a newspaper advertisement for a job, a Quebecer, a Torontonian and a Newfoundlander. Each one was interviewed separately and had to meet certain qualifications. They were interviewed in this order—the Quebecer, the Torontonian and the Newfoundlander.

However, there was one question which each one was asked and if he did not answer correctly he was eliminated.

They were to fill in the last word in this line: "Old MacDonald had a ——." The Quebecer's answer was house and the Torontonian's answer was barn. Of course they were both eliminated.

When the interviewer came to the Newfoundlander he said, "Well, all Newfoundlanders are smart fellas, surely you can answer this question correctly. Old MacDonald had a ——?"

Examiner: "Right on! Now spell it."

Newfoundlander: "Horse."

Examiner: "Right on! Now spell it."

Newfoundlander: "E.I.E.I.O."

TRY SMILING

When the weather suits you not,
Try smiling.
When your coffee isn't hot,
Try smiling.
When your neighbours don't do right,
Or your relatives all fight,
Sure 'tis hard, but then you might
Try smiling.

Doesn't change a thing, of course
Just smiling.
But it cannot make them worse
Just smiling.
And it seems to help your case,
Brightens up a gloomy place,
Then, it sort o'rests your face—
Just smiling

WINNING BY DECEITFUL SUGGESTION

In the early days of "snipe" sailing in the 1940's at Long Pond, Manuels, I was a member of the club.

When it was too windy to sail, it was normal for members to sit around and chat. One of our ardent members was Dr. E.F. Moores. We called him Dinty. Whenever Dinty decided he wanted to win a race, he won it. He was a great favourite at the club. There were times when Dinty came first in a race but disqualified himself for some breach of the rules. This was done just to encourage some young member of the club who had come in second.

One Wednesday half holiday afternoon, Dinty was telling of a few humourous instances in his life. This particular afternoon, he told us one morning, he went to his surgery and occupying the waiting room were four young ladies whom he knew were not regular patients of his. Not long before this occurred, he had decided not to increase his practice by adding new patients.

So Dinty went into his surgery, picked up a magazine and read for about 10 minutes. He then looked at his watch and announced, "Ladies, I don't think that doctor is coming this morning. I wouldn't wait for him if I were you. I'm not going to wait." He then left his office and the four ladies did likewise. He boarded his car, drove around the block a few times and returned to his office.

NO DOUBT EMBARRASSING

A kind and humble priest in our island had been in the parish of a rural district for many years. He was looked upon almost as a part of every family in the parish. He knew them all by their first names because he had christened most of them and saw them grow up. He was truly respected and loved. This affection was in return for the care and kindness he had shown his parishioners.

On one occasion however, an area of his humility backfired slightly. From time to time a new housekeeper was engaged and in his desire to have them feel a part of his household, he told each one not to refer to things about the residence as his but 'our'. For instance, they were to refer to the cooking stove, the refrigerator, or carpet as 'our' not 'your'.

This particular day the priest had a fellow priest in his study when the rather young housekeeper carried this "our" business, in her excitement, a bit too far. She rushed into the study out of breath and exclaimed,

"OH FATHER FATHER THERE'S A MOUSE UNDER OUR BED!"

THE REVEREND GEORGE EARLE

The Reverend George Earle, who has no equal, makes many after-dinner speeches and he states, "I can manage to hold a crowd if I give a talk on just what I call Newfoundlandia." He continues, "You can illustrate by just the natural expressions of some people who did not know they were funny, but their way of saying it by metaphor and simile and in other ways, is really funny."

He told this story which exemplifies what he is saying. I am going to tell it in his own words. "There was another old customer, he was mentioned in the *Squid Jiggin' Ground* song, Jacob Steele. Jacob was an odd bird on Change Islands. He didn't associate much with others. He used to think a lot. It was probably deep thinking. He was always thinking about the meaning of life and different things.

"He was an unusual customer. He didn't go to church and this was very rare in the old community. Jacob didn't go. They kept pressing him you know, and he didn't want to go until he was sure of it. He wanted to know what he was worshipping—and this is a man without any formal education whatsoever.

"Well, we had a doctor who was an unbeliever. But he was a good doctor. People sort of overlooked this, this queer thing that he was an unbeliever. So one day Jacob, who had been doing his thinking over the years, met the doctor and he says, 'Doctor, they tell me you don't believe in God.' And the doctor said, 'Well, it's not that I don't believe, I'm not sure and I haven't given much thought to it.'

"Then Jacob said, 'I've given a lot of thought to it you see, and now in me old age I've come to a conclusion and I see it this way. I think I should believe in God because, if you believe in God and you dies, and there's narn, you won't know anything about it anyway, and if you dies and there is one you'll be alright. But, if you don't believe and dies and finds there is one you'll be in one hell of a mess.' "

SICK, TIRED AND NOT TOO WELL

I'll begin by telling you a short story. In Riverhead, St. Mary's, I had a beautiful old friend. She was the wife of my guide Peter Lee. Well Mrs. Marie had arthritis for many years, but she knew if she didn't fight it she would become a victim and be a cripple—so fight it she did. Anyway, one leg persisted in losing much of its circulation and became permanently cool. She used to say that if she couldn't see it she did not know where it was—no feeling in it.

Her language was always very descriptive with a little humour thrown in. She was one of the old old school and did not believe that women smoked. On one occasion it was proven to her without doubt that a certain woman had been smoking while in bed and had caught the house on fire. When it eventually got through to Mrs. Lee that it was true she burst forth with:

"Blessed Virgin! 'Tis a pity almighty God didn't put her mouth back of her ear."

PENGUINS ENJOY THE ZOO

Here we are laughing at ourselves again.

This story takes place in Ontario. A driver of a transport truck suddenly found his vehicle inoperable. For an hour or more he tried to signal other drivers that he was in trouble. At last a transport truck of the same size as his stopped. The driver was a Newfoundlander.

When he walked up to the Ontario driver he said, "What's d'matter wid you old cock?"

The reply was, "Well my truck has broken down and I got a real problem. On board are 200 penguins which I am taking to the zoo in Toronto, and I can't leave them here on the highway and go looking for help."

The Newfoundlander solved the problem by suggesting, "Look 'ere, my truck is as big as yours; let's put 'em all in my truck and I'll take 'em to d'zoo fer yez."

So it was agreed. They transferred the penguins from one truck to the other. Then the Ontario chap took out a roll of paper money and gave the Newfoundlander $250 to take the penguins to the zoo.

About 10 o'clock that night the Ontario chap saw the Newfoundlander coming up Yonge Street with the 200 penguins following him. In his amazement he went up to the Newfoundlander and said, "Look here, I gave you $250 to take these penguins to the zoo!"

The Newfoundlander replied, "Dat's right b'y. Yes, and I had some change left over. They enjoyed the zoo so now I'm takin' 'em to the movies."

FISH OR NO FISH

An expression quite common throughout Newfoundland in years gone by, whether in jest or not, was "Fish or no fish I'll 'ave 'er in d'fall."

Well, on one occasion very recently a young couple made up their minds one Saturday morning that they would be married today, right this afternoon.

They approached first the captain at the Salvation Army Corps. He asked for their marriage licence but they could not produce it. He said it was against the law to marry them without a licence and he would have to refuse them. This was a revoltin' development for sure, because this was one obstacle that had not crossed their minds.

They thought they should examine all areas and next they tried their luck with the H'Anglican priest and, being turned down there, they approached the United Church Minister. No go! The three men of the church gave them the same answer—No licence, no marriage.

But not to be daunted they went back to the Salvation Army captain. The answer was again no and when the captain appeared to be a little upsot with them, the male hopeful came out with, "Ah come on now captain, you know you can say a few words jest to get us over the weekend."

IDENTITY CRISIS

There is a story which I would much rather tell than record it as I am doing here.

A government official had to interview a few people in one of the outports. When he arrived there he went to one of the homes to make some inquiries in order to locate the people he wished to talk with. His first question was:

Interviewer: "Is there a William Porter here?"

Resident: "No zir. No William Porter 'ere zir, no William Porter."

Interviewer: "What, no Bill Porter here?"

Resident: "Oh yes,.dere's a Bill Porter 'ere."

Interviewer: "How about John Kean?"

Resident: "No zir. No John Kean 'ere zir. No John Kean."

Interviewer: "What about Jack Kean?"

Resident: "Jack Kean? Jack Kean? Oh yes, sure dat's me."

NOT TRUE?

A visitor to Newfoundland was in St. John's and went into one of the restaurants on Duckworth Street. The waitress offered him a menu and then went about her other duties.

He had not seen on the menu what he wished to have. He looked at the waitress and asked,

"Pardon me, but do you have frogs legs?"

Waitress: "No zir, Dat's me 'igh heels makes me walk dat way."

HAPPY RETURNS?

Two neighbours had the habit of talking over the family doings as they held up the fence each morning.

Says one to her friend, "And why are ye sportin' a black eye this marnin' dearie?"

The other: "My husband came home from the penitentiary in Sin Jan's yesterday."

The first: "And what happened?"

The other: "Oh, it was his birthday and I wished him many happy returns."

MISCONCEPTION

The following story was told to me recently by a sister of the Catholic Church.

A visiting priest was having confession in a community where there was a convent. The sisters in this convent had a commitment of caring for orphan children and temporary care of children from broken homes. The number of children varied considerably from time to time.

One of the Sisters went to confession when there was this visiting priest in attendance. The sister on this occasion lost her balance as she entered the confessional. She knocked over the kneeling stool and caused quite a rumpus in doing so.

During her confession she included telling about times when she was impatient and cross with the children. The priest asked her how many children she had, and she replied, forty two. The priest reacted: "Get out! Get out! You're drunk. I knew you were drunk when you came in here."

A WUNERFUL BAD BACK

There is something we all do well in Newfoundland and that is, we use certain terminology in our everyday work outside and apply to our life indoors, or should we say our life at home.

Visiting Catalina about six or seven years ago, I met the Anglican priest who told me a very funny story about one of his parishioners.

He was called to visit a lady who had had a bad fall and in doing so injured her back. It resulted in her having to stay in bed for several months.

After two months, he was making his regular call, and was surprised to find her downstairs in the kitchen. Well he told her how happy he was to find her so much improved, and then remarked, "The next thing we'll be seeing you in church," and she replied, "No Riverend no. I don't t'ink so cuz me back eh's wunerful, wunerful bad. I git's in d'bid an' I can't turn h'over. I 'aves to git out of bid, go down along d'side of 'n, go cross d'h'end and git in d'hudder side."

The reverend's comment then was, "I s'pose your husband has to do the same thing?"

"No zir no. Eh juss sheaves astern."

THE NEGATIVE HELD THE CLUE

It is a habit of mine as I drive along, to recognize people by a wave of my hand, whether I know them or not. One day this produced a great story.

I was parking my car on Empire Avenue and I waved to a fellow who was carrying an orange garbage bag on his back. He approached me and said:

"You're Al Clouston?"

I replied, "Yes, and I'll bet you are spellin' that bag down to the cemetery."

He replied, "Oh my! I never heard that word since me fouder died."

And then he continued on: "It was only last week I said to my wife, 'If Al Clouston had this story'."

I asked him to tell me the story and he did.

In Island Cove a fella died. His brudder Tom was wunerful concarned cuz Joe died and Tom had nider picture of 'n. Well eh was some upsot. About two years passed and Tom's wife found a small snapshot of Joe covered up in a drawer. She went right downstairs and said, "Tom, look what I got," and she showed him the snapshot. Tom's reaction was, "DAT'S EH! DAT'S EH! But eh's wunerful small idn't eh? I'll take'n over to Mr. Tooton's now an' eh'll make 'n biggah."

Tom took the snapshot over to Tooton's and he was told that it would be no trouble at all to enlarge brudder Joe.

Just before he left the store he turned around and said to Mr. Tooton,

SIMPLE THINKING THOUGH DISASTROUS

An alcoholic, who had a long and varied experience with the stuff, decided for himself to seek some help. He went to his regular physician who knew this patient very well.

First of all the doctor gave him a considerable amount of advice. Then he gave the man a complete physical examination to discover what inroads the alcohol had made on its victim over the years. When the interview had started the doctor felt the man's hearing was noticeably impaired and on examination he confirmed for himself that this was true. So the doctor advised him that if he didn't stop drinking he would go completely deaf.

Six months went by before our patient made his next visit to his doctor. The man's hearing had become considerably worse. So with some impatience the doctor said to him, "Look here Harry, can't you do better than this and try to give up your drinking? I told you you would go deaf."

And Harry's reply was, "Well, Doc b'y, I'll tell ya d'way it is. I likes what I drinks more den what I hears."

SELF-INFLICTED

Many service clubs have after-dinner speakers from time to time.

I have been a member of the Kinsmen Club for many years. About 1951, a year or so after Confederation in Newfoundland, Dr. Leonard Miller came to our club to speak to us and gave us some idea of the Government Health Plans which were being suggested. At one point in his talk he said if a certain plan was implemented, it would pay for everything except maternity. One of our members asked:

"Why not maternity, Dr. Miller?"

And before Dr. Miller could answer, a member of our club, lawyer Bill Adams, yelled out:

"BECAUSE 'TIS SELF-INFLICTED."

SOCKED IN BUT NOT IN FOG

As a rule, when anyone says, "Al, did you hear about the Newfoundlander who—" usually I do just that, I cut him off in the middle of his sentence. Recently however, I did stop and the story was this.

A young Newfoundlander, fifteen years old, went to Toronto for ten days and his mother told him to put on clean socks everyday . . . the last day there, he couldn't get his boots on.

PIECE OF HIS MIND

A very promising student of the literary and debating class left a small community in Newfoundland and headed out for greener fields. It was not too long before news drifted back home about his success as a writer for a mainland paper. After a number of years he became a noted columnist for one of the leading periodicals.

Now the clergyman back home who admired this successful columnist as a student, was not too pleased with the content of his articles as a writer.

It took many years for the "local boy makes good" to return to the community where he was born. The same clergyman was still reigning. When he met the student, twenty years and more had passed since they had seen one another. At the first opportunity the clergyman said, "Look here Will, I've waited a long time to give you a piece of my mind."

Before the clergyman could say anything further the successful student said, "Be careful now Reverend, at your age you don't have much to spare."

NOT HIS FAULT

One morning last year I met a friend in Churchill Square whom I had not seen for several years. His name is John Walsh. (How many John Walsh's are there?) John is the type who says it as it is and in such a way that it always comes out humourous and with no offense.

We entered the Giant Mart and the lady at the first cash register was obviously very pregnant. As we passed her, John leaned towards her and said, "Ah! You can't blame me this time." The lady, John and I broke into howls of laughter and only the three of us could enjoy the humour of it. It goes to prove that the best humour happens in everyday life and on the spur of the moment.

GUILTY ONE WAY OR THE OTHER

The following humorous incident did take place but not in Newfoundland.

In June I attended the "Citizen of Year" Dinner at the Newfoundland Hotel. The appointing of this honourable individual is always sponsored by the J.C.'s. This year their special speaker for the day was the President of the Bar Association of Canada.

He told a story about a court case which took place in Western Canada. It is so similar to a Ted Russell story that it is worth recording.

A man stole a horse. The individual from whom the horse was stolen was rather a detestable character which nobody cared much about. The trial was held before a Jury and the Judge told them there was no doubt about the verdict they should bring in.

The Jury was only out an hour when they returned.

Judge: Have you reached a verdict?

Foreman: Yes, your honour. Not guilty, but the accused must return the horse.

Well the Judge was furious and he sent the Jury back out. In a very short time the Jury returned again.

Judge: Have you reached a verdict?

Foreman: Yes your honour. Guilty, but the accused can keep the horse.

OLD TIME FUNERALS

Not too long ago I heard a story about a wake. In this case, preparations got going early. The husband had been ill for several years and the doctor had visited regularly. This particular day the doctor found the patient in a much weakened condition and remarked to the wife that her husband would probably die today.

She got a big pot of soup going and about 10 o'clock at night made a visit upstairs. The first thing her poor husband had to say was,

PRACTICAL JOKING

In 1977 the Canadian Managing Editors Conference was held in Newfoundland. I was engaged to speak at one of the luncheons to give the visitors a taste of our Newfoundland humour. One visitor, Ray Timson of the *Toronto Star,* called me to his table and said, "You have the most original and Canadian humour I have heard for a long time. Do you know why Al? Because nobody stayed up half the night dreaming it up."

He made a request for me to contact him when next in Toronto and said, "I want you to have lunch with me and three of my top editors." He was as good as his word and we had lunch at the Quo Vadis Restaurant.

They listened to me for awhile and then I heard some of their humour. A practical joke I heard about at the luncheon was this:

A very "well-do-do" Florida resident who was always playing practical jokes on his friends, needed another small car along with his other cars. One of his friends thought he should buy a Volkswagon which he did.

The friend thought this would be a good time to repay the new owner of the Volkswagon for the practical jokes of which he was the recipient. The friend on each night for a week, had someone fill up the Volkswagon's gas tank almost to the top. For all that week the owner of the Volkswagon went about boasting about getting seventy miles to the gallon from his new car. The next week the friend had someone pump out gas from the gas tank of the Volks. Then the Volks dropped to ten miles to the gallon.

You can imagine the owner and the agent for the Volks trying to solve the mystery until his friend came forward with the answer.

I can see someone in Newfoundland taking a cue from this practical joke and doing the same thing.

AN EXPENSIVE FISHING EXPEDITION

As most people know, the Gander River has been famous for salmon fishing. For years now, guides have been available to fishing parties from other parts of Canada and the United States.

An American from New York arranged a fishing party. He had the guide meet him and his party from New York at Gander. They visited some of the choice fishing pools on the Gander River and a week later returned to Gander to get their flight back to New York.

The leader of the party had been only partially successful. He had caught only one salmon. As you can imagine, to come to Newfoundland for a week's fishing is quite expensive. The leader was not very backward in letting his listeners know his disappointment and how much it had all cost him.

While waiting for his flight, he went about the airport lobby announcing loudly in a very American accent: "ONE FISH, $2,000, THAT'S A LOT OF MONEY FOR ONE FISH, $2,000."

After an elderly Newfoundlander had heard this several times he got close to the American and said, "You're lucky, you didn't catch two."

WHAT A SQUATTIN'

I have many Roman Catholic friends and the fun never stops, for we are always making good-natured jokes about our respective faiths. I heard something similar the other day.

Dan was watching his friend approach and thought he would have some fun.

Dan: "Lookut Mickey, did ya hear d'news?"

Mickey: "What news?"

Dan: "Oh, the bottom fell out of purgatory last night, and all the Catholics went to hell."

Mickey: "Oh, God help the poor Protestants. What a squattin' they must have got."

HE WAS RIGHT

An American had come to Port aux Basques with his motor home. He was on the highway about 10 miles when he thought about the fact that he had not paid much attention to the highway signs and probably he was not on the correct road to St. John's.

He pulled into the side of the road where one of the locals was standing and he asked the question, "Am I on the right road to St. John's?"

The reply, "Yes me zon, you're on the right road to St. John's, and stop at d'second light cuz you're dere."

A MIRACLE

A resident of the Southern Shore up Ferryland way, had heard all the young people talking about their wonderful travels to Florida, California, Mexico and all over. After listening to this for a few years he also got the wander lust and decided to make his way to Mexico.

He enjoyed his two weeks there and the Tequila helped a lot. He liked it so much that he bought a forty ouncer to take home with him. But he was not going to pay any duty if he could get away with it. So he thought he would pull a fast one, so he poured the Tequila in a plain glass bottle.

On the American border his baggage was examined and the American customs man came across the bottle and said, "hey, man, what do we have here?" In his beautiful Southern Shore accent the Newfoundlander replied, "Howly Water, Howly Water." The American opened the bottle and took a sip and exclaimed, "Hey man, this is Tequila!" "The Lard be praised!" cried the Newfoundlander, "Shur 'tis a MIRACLE, 'TIS A MIRACLE!"

AN EXCELLENT IDEA

Last year, a team of young people went to play soccer in England. One of the team was telling his parents about the trip and said that he went into a large department store and signs were quite prominent in all areas of the store which read, "SHOPLIFTERS WILL BE KILLED AND EATEN."

EMBARRASSING MEAT

We can all remember when we were young fellas how we would be invited to stay to our friend's house to dinner or supper.

A boy or nine was asked to stay to dinner and was having quite a struggle cutting through the meat. Wishing to be helpful his friend's mother said, "pass your plate to me Jim and I'll cut your meat for you."

The reply, "no mam, tis alright. We have it just as tough as this at home."

MUSHROOMS FOR DOGS ONLY

A lady who owned a farm noticed, at a certain location, that mushrooms had been appearing for several years. They got more numerous year after year. She began to wonder if they were the edible variety or not. Well, without consulting anyone who would know she decided on a plan. She would cook some of these mushrooms, mix them with some meat and feed them to the dog. If the dog survived why not humans?

She proceeded with the plan. She fed the mixture to the dog, waited several days and noticed that the dog had no ill effects.

Some months later she threw a dinner party and served these mushrooms to her guests. The main course was over and things were going fine, when the maid quietly approached the lady of the house, who was sitting at the table, and whispered these words, "The dog is dead." The hostess did not wait to hear anymore from the maid. She launched into an explanation about the mushrooms, became very excited, and had two doctors come immediately to her home and had stomach pumps used on the guests.

The operation was completed and again the maid quietly approached the hostess and said, "Madame, the man who ran over your dog came and took it away."

WORMS ARE EXTRA

Talking to a man from out in the bay, who now resides in St. John's, he told me about one trip when, while visiting "over 'ome," he bought some fish. When he was about to cook it he discovered that the fish had worms in it.

The next day he went to a fish store in St. John's and bought some more cod fish. The clerk wrapped it and as it was being handed to him he remarked,

SECOND THE MOTION

A German, a Frenchman and a Newfoundlander all applied for the same job. A question which they all had to answer before either one of them could qualify for the job was: how many seconds were there in a year?

The German was going to use his computer, the Frenchman was going to use his mental arithmetic, but the Newfoundlander was faster than either one of the other two. He replied immediately:

"Nuttin' to dat b'y. Twelve."

"TWELVE?" said the interviewer.

"Yes b'y, second of January, second of February . . . second of December . . ."

FRESH OR FROZE

A couple of years ago, just after Christmas, I visited my relatives at Halliday's Butcher Shop. They told me that they were waiting for me to come in to tell me a true story.

A customer had come into the shop during the Christmas season and asked for two birds. One of the boys asked the question, "Do you want them fresh or frozen?"

The reply, "Oi h'eats nuttin' froze. Froze takes d'tas'e h'off ut. Oi believes h'ol man it h'even takes d'tas'e h'off d' h'ice cream."

ILLNESS IS INCONVENIENT

A couple who had lived an average life found themselves back where they had started from. They had raised a large family but had been careful with their income and were now independent.

For a number of years they made trips to see their offspring on the mainland, and when at home took in all the local social events and parties. This going slowed up eventually because the husband became chronically ill. Just as they were about to start on another escapade he would become ill which foiled their plans. His partner was not taking too kindly to this inconvenient illness because she was missing out on the fun and it was not her fault.

One night he became unconscious and she sent for the doctor. When the doctor arrived he took one look at the patient and whispered to the wife, "I believe he's dead." The doctor went to the other side of the room to take off his coat. At the same time the husband opened his eyes and said,

YOU HAVE TO IMAGINE IT FOR YOURSELF

Here is a story where you have to use your imagination. As the story was being told to me I was visualizing every move and I laughed heartily.

It was back in the days when Newfoundlanders were very apt in entertaining themselves with practical jokes.

Two fellows went across the bay in a boat to visit some friends. They had no difficulty going over for there was only a light breeze of wind on the water.

However, when they decided to start for home the wind had come up and it was too loppy for them to go home.

The decision was made to stay the night and the two visitors were assigned to sleep in the kitchen. Well, the one who had had too much to drink decided to get himself horizontal on a very short couch which was in the kitchen. He lay down and was unconscious in no time. The couch was so short that he lay on his back with his feet touching the floor.

His buddy thought he would have some fun. He got some fishin' line and wound it around his friend and the couch, thereby fastening his friend solidly to the couch.

He next got the 12-gauge gun, took the shot out of a cartridge, placed it in the gun and fired it off.

Well, his friend on the couch suddenly came to life with a livin' leap and started prancing around the kitchen with the couch on his back. But, in firing off the gun he had set fire to the curtains.

The next thing to happen was a very natural one. The noise from the gun had awakened everyone in the house and they all came into the kitchen to see a very confused situation. Buddy was going mad around the kitchen with the couch on his back and the house was on fire.

The first thing to be done was to put out the fire. Then they relieved Buddy of his load of couch. When the architect of the prank explained what he had conceived they put on the kettle to have a cup of tea and loaf, and all hands had a good laugh.

To many, I know, it sounds an incredible story, but not to me. Given the same set of circumstances I would be capable of performing the same mischief.

MOST NATURAL FOR A CAT

As I always tell my audience, nonsense and fabrications are always the best entertainers. Here is a story which illustrates such a statement.

Visiting Twillingate, I met a resident who invited me to his home. He was eighty-five years of age and was a most interesting person to talk to. Since he had read the funny stories in my books he thought I should hear the following.

A man who had lost his sight visited the hospital. He had heard of transplants of hearts, kidneys and other organs of the body, so why not eyes?

He was told at the hospital that it wasn't impossible to do eye transplants just yet but they were getting close to doing it. He was to come back in six months time.

He went back in six months time and was told that it was now possible to do transplants of eyes but they had no human eyes at present. But, if he was willing, they had cats' eyes which they could give him. The man figured that any eyes were better than no sight at all.

The hospital proceeded with the transplants and the patient received two cats' eyes. Bandages were applied covering his new eyes, of course, and he was warned not to remove them for ten days—remove them then and he would have his sight.

He did as he was told, and after ten days, his daughter removed the bandages. The man looked all over the kitchen and then got down on the floor and crawled under the stove.

NECESSARY DISCIPLINE

A student in the class was not giving enough attention while lectures were in progress. Also, his assignments had not been researched and were far below the standard required. Eventually, the teacher decided that it was time to advise his parents of the situation, so she made a phone call to his home and his mother answered the phone call.

A discussion took place and at a certain point the teacher made an observation.

Teacher: He's bright and he tries, but I'm going to have to discipline him because he spends too much time chasing the girls.

Mother: Good. Let me know how it works and I'll try it on his father.

ANGELS FLY?

"Do angels fly mother?"

"Yes dear."

"Then when is nursie going to fly, cause Daddy called her angel last night."

"I can tell you now, she'll fly tomorrow."

NO OTHER ALTERNATIVE

Before the days of automobiles and trucks, all Her Majesty's mail was carried by water to various areas of our coast. Settlements which were accessible by horse and wagon received theirs in this alternate manner. The Southern Shore was one of these areas, and mail and newspapers only went up the shore twice or three times a week.

A story which I was told originated in Ferryland and goes like this: A man went into the general store and made an announcement in very loud and direct terms—

Customer: I wants d'newspaper.

Owner: Do y'want yisteidy's or t'days?

Customer: I wants t'days.

Owner: Well, y'll have t'wait 'til tamarra.

SOME STUNNED!

One day last week my young newspaper delivery boy said to me, "Here is a story for you. Did you hear about the mainlander who locked his keys in the car?"

I replied, "No, you tell me about him."

"It took him three days to get his wife and children out!"

AGE MAKES NO DIFFERENCE

I think I have mentioned this before, that it is a delight to answer the telephone and find that the caller has gotten a wrong number. Last Saturday I got a wrong number call about 10:30 am.

Me: Well?

Caller: Is Paula there?

Me: How old is she?

Caller: About twenty-two.

Me: I'm seventy-five so she is just my size.

Caller: Well, b'y, if I find her I'll send her down to you.

Then we both laughed for about a minute without saying anything more. We did not identify ourselves. When he stopped laughing he said, "Hear you again some time."

I said, "Proper ting," and we both hung up.

It is such a mistake not to take the opportunity each day to have some fun. President Eisenhower said, "The day you don't have fun, it is not only unnecessary, it is unchristian."

GOVAMENT 'WARRVES'

When the champions of Confederation were travelling in 1948 and 1949, they painted a glowing picture of what Newfoundland would become as the result of our becoming a province of Canada. True, many of the promises came to pass and all the basic things that were to come to us through Confederation with Canada, did come.

But the champions of the cause which I mentioned in the foregoing were too enthusiastic and many exaggerations of the benefits went a bit too far.

After Confederation became a fact, many letters containing requests and fulfillment of promises were addressed to Mr. Smallwood 'eeself. Just a note aside, very recently I heard of a sawmill owner who, hearing Mr. Smallwood's name mentioned, bellowed forth: "JOEY! Eef oi 'ad 'en 'ere right now I'd make small wood of 'en."

Anyway, many letters requested a govament 'warrf'. It was evident that one of these 'warrves' was necessary in most communities whether there were 1,000 families or 10 or 12 families there. After all, this was one of the promises.

A school friend of mine became an employee of the provincial government in the early days of Confederation. One of his duties was to have the laborious task, but also amusing, of sorting out the requests in these letters which were worth considering.

He told me about one letter which was wirtten direct to Mr. Smallwood 'eeself, and is as follows:

"Dear Mr. Smallwood,

Since youse a told me yerself lass year we wuz to git a govament warrf, weez writin' now to mind youse 'bout it. We fellers never 'ad nar warrf cartny, an' h'everyt'ing comed 'ere be d'coastal boat we fellers 'ad to go out in boat an' ketch en as eh wuz slung h'over d'side of 'er as eh come down. An' sometimes Mr. Smallwood zir we 'aves a carpse come 'ome to be buried an' eh falls in d'arbour water. An' Mr. Smallwood zir youse knows dat's no way to treat a carpse."

NINETY NINE YEARS

When the Second World War broke out the face of many areas of Newfoundland changed considerably. One area was the farmland to the east of St. John's. What was known as Ross's farm and Woodley's farm was the land which the United States purchased to build a headquarters and training corps for their operations in Newfoundland. The area was known as Fort Pepperell. Argentia became a U.S. Naval base and at Stephenville the U.S. built an air force base. These bases were leased to the U.S. for 99 years.

This all came about through an agreement between Churchill and Roosevelt. England needed war ships. The United States had war ships in mothballs. The deal was made that the United States would get bases in Newfoundland and in return the U.S. would supply fifty destroyers to England.

About six months after Fort Pepperell was established an American Army truck stopped near the Railway station in St. John's West and the driver told a city fellow he was having difficulty finding the Southside Road. The American soldier was given the information to get him to his destination, but our city man added, "You've got nuttin' to worry about b'y, cuz you've got 99 years to find it."

SHORT ON WORDS

A father, who had seen all his family grow up and leave home to settle far off on the mainland, decided it was time he made a visit to see how they were all doing. Someone arranged a passage for him on Air Canada and he joined the flight in Gander.

He was a man who had not travelled very far outside his own community and had developed a wariness of strangers. He was a man of few words anyway, and he decided that on this trip not to be drawn into conversation with any of his fellow travellers.

His destination was Toronto. The flight arrived at Malton and within a short time all passengers were crowding about the carousel, but for half an hour no luggage made its appearance. (So what else is new?) Everyone was becoming impatient. A passenger, who was standing right by our visiting father, tried to draw him into conversation, but all he got was one syllable replies. Eventually he asked, "Here all your life?" And our Newfoundlander replied grudgingly, "I hope not!"

THE WEDDIN'

About a month ago I talked about old-time Newfoundland weddings, and which in some areas were successful events if they ended up in a fight. Well this following short story demonstrates the anticipation of the events to come.

A young fellow met his friend and said, "Is ya goin' to d'weddin' tonight?"

"What weddin'?"

"Our Suse is gettin' married tonight b'y."

"Where's it to?"

"Weddin' is up in d'chapel, d'toime is in our kitchen, and d'fight is in Uncle Tom's garden."

A MATTER OF INSURANCE

An old lady was very disturbed about losing her diamond ring. She told all her family about it and then suddenly remembered it was insured. She contacted the insurance agent and told him the circumstances under which she had lost it. It was quite apparent to him that the ring was only mislaid but after about three months the company was under considerable pressure and paid her the $1,200.00.

The company asked her to keep an eye out for the ring and advise them. Another three months went by and the insurance agent came around to see her. He asked her if she had found the diamond ring and she replied, "Oh my yes, I found the ring and I did not think it was right for me to keep the ring and the money, so I sent the $1,200.00 to the Red Cross."

NEWFOUNDLANDERS

During the war boom in Newfoundland, American foremen and superintendents were appalled that a man would leave a good job, just to be at home for a few months. There was moose huntin' and birdin' to be done too. These Americans did not know that Newfoundlanders "went home in the fall."

An Irishman, an American and a Newfoundlander all arrived at the gate of heaven at the same time. St. Peter addressed the Irishman first and asked his nationality. He was told to take the first train north and he would get to the community where all the Irishmen were congregated. St. Peter directed the American to take the next train south.

When St. Peter came to the Newfoundlander he said "Where do you belong?"

"Newfoundland," was the reply. And St. Peter said, "My son you'd better stay right here by the gate because you'll want to go home in the fall."

MORE ABOUT WAKES

A few weeks ago I wrote about wakes in Newfoundland. I explained that in some communities a wake became an event, and not only the people of the locality came to take in the excitement, but people in the whole area would come.

Last week a reader who agreed with me sent in the following:

A fellow who had left home to travel to the wake, arrived home after several days very much the worse for wear. He was truly worn out and had a few scars. (A funeral was equal to a wedding in those bygone days, even including the fight.) However, when he was asked how he had enjoyed the wake, he braced himself and sat up as if he was the victor and said, "We sure had d' devil's own toime b'y, dere was only one sound nose in d' bloody place and dat belonged to d' tay kittle."

HOMESICK SALESMAN

A Newfoundland salesman on a business trip across the island, went into a restaurant and ordered his breakfast.

Salesman: "Bring me uncooked bacon, wet scrambled eggs, burnt toast and weak coffee."

Waitress: "Anything else sir?"

Salesman: "Yes, sit down and grumble at me, I'm homesick."

BIBLE NAMES

The visiting evangelist had preached for nearly an hour and a half. He had gone through the prophets in the Old Testament and talked about them one by one. Suddenly he said:

"AND NOW WE COME TO JEREMIAH. WHAT WILL WE DO WITH JEREMIAH?" A man in the back row stood up and said, "HE CAN HAVE MY SEAT REVEREND. I'M JUST ABOUT TO LEAVE."

BIG MISTAKES

A doctor on the Southern Shore, about 50 years ago, had one of his patients build a slide for him. After using it all winter getting logs to his residence from in the country, the slide started to come apart in places where it should not have. It would have to be rebuilt for sure.

The doctor met the builder who made the slide and said, "Look here, you did not do a good job when you made that slide. It has come apart in many places. There is no trouble to see where you made your big mistakes and covered them with putty and paint."

The man thought for a moment and replied, "Yes doctor, 'tis somethin' like yerself, except you cover your big mistakes with the pick and shovel."

BELIEVE IT OR NOT

A credible story which is really a Newfoundland "Believe It Or Not," is a story about a woman who died twice but on her first trip to the graveyard did not make the grave. I said credible because the man who told me had a man with him who vouched for the truth of the tale. It happened about 60 years ago.

Apparently, a woman died in one of the communities in the bay. The woman was waked in the church and the religious service was held on the day of the proposed burial. The coffin was placed on a horsedrawn wagon to the gate of the cemetery. Six pallbearers removed the coffin from the wagon and proceeded to carry it through the gate opening. Going through the opening the coffin was knocked heavily against one of the gate posts. Immediately a noise was heard coming from within the coffin. The cover was unfastened and to everyone's amazement the woman was alive.

She was taken back home by her husband and was soon doing her normal housekeeping. She lived on for 20 years and then died a second time.

As she was being carried through the gate on this occasion a pallbearer was heard to remark, "Now b'ys don't knock 'er agin' the gate this time."

SICK TIRED AND NOT TOO WELL

The Gerald S. Doyle News Bulletin was a great service to the Newfoundland people, especially the outport people. It broadcast many messages of all kinds. A sample was the hospital report which gave people back home a report on how their relatives were making out in hospital, a report on their progress and when they expected to be discharged from the hospital. The patients also enjoyed hearing about themselves.

One particular patient who had been in hospital for ten days and did not hear his name mentioned on the radio decided that tomorrow he would do something about it.

He was up early the next morning and, walking in the corridor, he met Dr. Pat Whelan and said, "Pardon me now zir but is youse a doctah?"

Pat said yes he was and our patient continued, "Well doctah my name is Billy Jones. Glad to talk wid ya zir. Good-bye now."

That night Pat Whalen was listening to the Doyle message news and he heard a special from Billy Jones to his family, "Saw doctor today. Feelin' fine."

TALL TALE

The general store was more than a place just to acquire all the necessities of life. It was a meeting place, a news room and a place to hear yarns, certainly. One prominent writer of Newfoundland told me about his father's store. It was a club and he had heard hundreds of stories, but had never written down one, and then he said, "and you looking in from the outside Al, saw what a wonderful wealth of folklore humour we had in the outports and started to record it in voice, and writing about it."

Here's more nonsense which gives the greatest laughs. One is trying to outdo the other.

Sitting in the general store two oldtimers were doing just that. The first contestant said, "I 'ad a relative who wuz so fass eh'd 'ave d'fellers shoot at 'n and den outrun d' bullet be five mile."

Then his friend said "You t'inks dat's fass, Lookut, I'd a cousin who could blow out d' lamp an' den be undressed an' in bid afore d'room got dark."

A REVOLTIN' DEVELOPMENT TO BE SURE

Two fellows who belonged to King's Cove, B.B., were laid off from Buchans. After a day or two they decided to return home to King's Cove. Before they left Buchans they were half shot and by the time they arrived home in King's Cove they were ossified.

The next day neither one of them remembered going to the wake which was in progress when they arrived home. But one will always remember being at the wake because when he awoke the next morning he found himself in the same room with the carpse.

The carpse was horizontal in the coffin and our friend was horizontal on the couch parallel to the carpse. After boozing all the day previous you can imagine he wasn't feeling very good. He had a big head-plus.

After recovering from the shock of seeing the coffin, he eventually stood up and made the motion to leave the room, but before doing so, he went back, and looking down, he said to the carpse, "I don't know how you're feelin' but it got to be a heck of a sight better than the way I'm feelin'."

CHILDREN SAY THE DARNEDEST THINGS

A superintendent of a Sunday school had to substitute one Sunday morning for a teacher who was absent. He kept asking questions of the children and eventually asked:

"Where does God live?"

"In the bathroom in our house."

In surprise the superintendent asked, "Why do you say that Jim?"

"Cuz every morning in our house, Dad comes and bangs on the bathroom door and shouts, 'GOOD LORD! ARE YOU STILL IN THERE,?"

A mother had finished reading a *Bible* story to her four-year-old daughter Jennifer. Then when Jennifer was in the bath she said, "Mommy, is God in this house?"

"Yes."

"Is He in this bathroom?"

"Yes."

"Is He in this bath?"

"Yes."

"Then Jennifer pulled the plug and said, "Oops! There He goes down the drain."

A GOOD REASON TO MOURN

He kept on repeating this over and over and the woman thought that the Christian thing to do was to go over to the man and attempt to console him. She did just that and when she got close to the man on his knees she said,

A PAINFUL EYE ACCIDENT

A son had travelled to St. John's with his father. His father had experienced a painful eye accident in the woods. The doctor in the area examined the man and advised he should go to St. John's but did not give his family much hope and said that the father would possibly lose his eye.

Three days passed and the son sent a message home via the Gerald S. Doyle News Bulletin. The message sounds better when read to you than when you read it yourself. However this was the message:

"Father had eye removed today. Father and I on train Friday."

INCONVENIENT FEELIN'

Father Coady from Tor's Cove who, when he became ill, could not get to St. John's. He phoned Dr. Joe Murphy and told him all his ailments. Poor Joe couldn't stop him for he went on and, and when he did finally halt to take a breath, Dr. Joe said, "Father Coady you've got me completely confused. Can't you tell me in a few chosen words how you feel?"

Father Coady replied, "Now Joe b'y, 'tis an inconvenient feelin' and when I goes to bed at night I can't get into a state of unconsciousness."

TRAIN GOING BROAD SIDES

The following story has been told about the first time the railway passed through various communities. The first time I heard it, I was assured it was said in Glenwood.

As you can imagine, the people in all communities through which the railway was to pass were waiting expectantly for its first arrival. One of the features of the train that rather appalled everyone was its length.

In Glenwood, when the excitement had died down and the train had passed on, the village humourist remarked, "Good thing she never came in broadsides or she'd 'ave sweeped Glenwood."

GET THIS FOR GRATITUDE

A very happy rescuer was being commended by people standing around the shore of the pond where he had just saved a little boy from drowning. Suddenly the attention of everyone was distracted by a very large and loud woman who was making her way towards the rescuer with her apron and hair flying in the wind.

Woman: Are you d'man who saved me b'y?

Rescuer: Yes mam, I am.

Woman: Well den, where's eh's cap?

WHAT DID HE SAY?

Years ago people made funny stabs at recalling and repeating what the doctor had named their particular disease or ailment, after they had made a visit to see him. They repeated what they thought they heard. For instance yellow jaundice was often referred to as "yaller ganders". Even today ulcers are called "H'ulsters". As one person put it "the shots they made at it were hilarious."

One day two fellows who were a little more educated than the average, were on the fishin' grounds and they thought they would have some fun. They were discussing "ol' Uncle Abe" whom they knew had diabetes.

The story was told to me this way.

Uncle Willy was fishin' close by and one of the guys cupped his hands around his gob and yelled, "Hey, Uncle Willy, what did the doctor say ailed poor old Abe?" Straightening up with a yank at his cap Willy yelled back "Eh got da Barbados."

"No Willy B'y. Not the Barbados," yelled back the other fellow in merriment, "Maybe it t'was diabetes?"

Willy not knowing really what his old friend Abey had, jumped up on the gangboards, hauled out his pipe and yelled, "Yes, b'y, dat's what I toll yees it 'twere, Barbados."

ELEPHANTS ARE NOT FOR TORONTO

A Newfoundlander was standing on the corner of College Street and Yonge for a whole week. He kept on clicking his fingers and saying "Keep out! Keep out! Don't come in here."

A Torontonian who had been hearing this each day as he passed became quite curious and asked the Newfoundlander what was he up to and the reply was "Keeping the elephants out of Toronto."

The Torontonian reacted quickly and said loudly, "MY DEAR MAN THERE IS NOT AN ELEPHANT WITHIN A THOUSAND MILES OF TORONTO."

So the Newfoundlander quietly said,

HIGH TEMPERATURE

Last Christmas I made a visit to a friend's home just as they were ready to sit down to dinner. I was made very welcome and was invited to stay and share in the meal.

The meal had to be well digested because laughs were plentiful. Everyone told a story or two.

One story that was passed onto me was by an Anglican minister who was from Labrador and was visiting St. John's for a few days.

It seems a young fellow of twenty had requested the doctor to come and visit his mother who was quite ill. But the problem was the doctor would have to leave the hospital and travel a distance of seven or eight miles to see this lady. He did not go and when he was talking to the son on the third phone call the doctor asked some questions and it did not appear that it was necessary for him to make the trip. But the boy was insisting and the doctor said, "Look here does she have a temperature?" The reply, "Temperature doctor? 'Er temperature wus so 'igh lass night it warped 'er false teet'."

JUST LIKE A BABY!

As we all know, in the past few years quite a number of business houses have found themselves in financial difficulty. Some have struggled through the crisis and now feel they will make it. One of these is a person we know well.

We were talking with him about it and mentioned what a worry it has been to him. Then one of the company of four asked him how he was sleeping, and his reply was, "Just like a baby . . . I sleep for two hours, wake up and cry for two hours."

Children often give their elders a laugh and the following is a sample:

"What are eyes for?" a child in kindergarten was asked.

"To see with."

"And your nose?"

"To smell with."

"And what are your ears for?"

"To keep clean."

EDUCATION

Royal Readers were the standard of education in Newfoundland in years gone by. If you asked a fellow what education he had he could reply that he left school in the third book or the fifth book, all this meant Royal Reader numbers and each number was an advancement in school.

There has been many stories told about those readers and the most famous one in my opinion was the one about Mr. Mouland of the Newfoundland Disaster.

Some federal people came to Newfoundland after Confederation and made a survey to determine the level of education we had on the island. Visiting with Mr. Mouland they asked him how long he had spent in school. "Well," he said, "I went to school and on my startin' day they were readin' from a book tellin' about Tom and his dog. Someone threw a stick out in the water and Tom's dog went after it and before the dog got back to shore I was out of school." That meant he had probably spent the most of one morning in school.

SO WHAT?

The following is supposed to be an authentic story from the Northern Peninsula.

A tourist drove up to the gas station and requested $5.00 worth of gas. When the gas started to flow onto the ground the tourist called out, "Hey! The gas is running onto the ground."

Young tank attendant: "Yes, but 'tis not $5.00 worth yet."

HE'S BETTER WHEN HE'S WORSE

A story from the west end of the city. Mrs. O'Brien and Mrs. Murphy were neighbours and spent many a morning hour leanin' on the fence discussing their family woes and of course the crumbs about the people in the neighbourhood.

Mr. Murphy had an accident some weeks before so Mrs. O'Brien asked Mrs. Murphy what was the state of her husband's health.

Mrs. Murphy replied, "Well gurl, I tell ya now. Sometimes he's better and sometimes he's worse. But the way he yells and swears when he's better I tink he's better when he's worse.

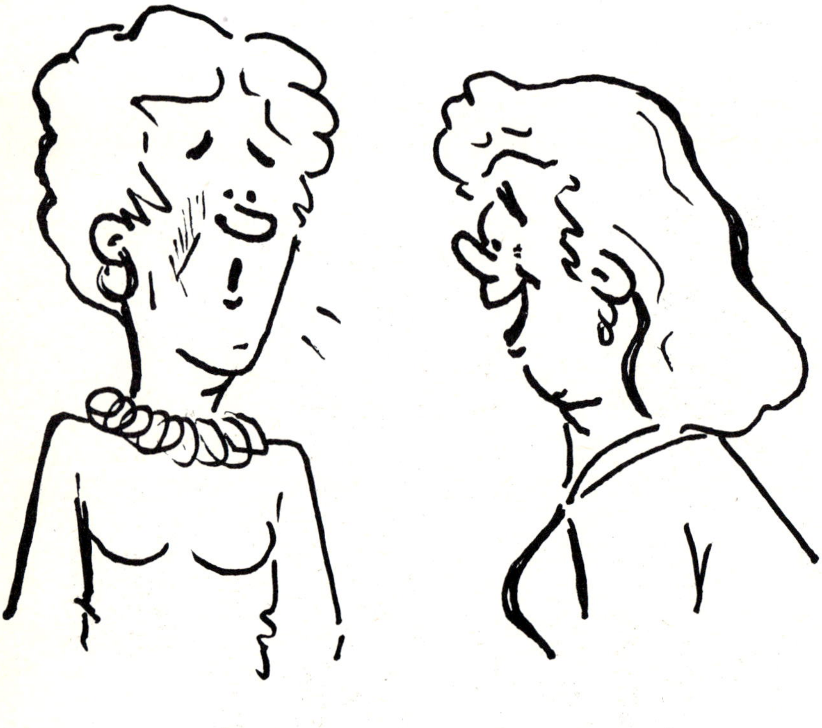

ONE HUNDRED YEARS OLD

About fifteen years ago, when I was the local president of the Canadian Bible Society, I was requested by the Secretary to go to St. Luke's Anglican Home for the aged to present a Bible to a certain gentleman on his birthday. This particular birthday was to be one which very few of the population reach. He was to become a centenarian, 100 years old.

When I arrived at St. Luke's, there were ten other people there to present their gifts. We all had a little speech to make, of course, but there was something none of us wellwishers knew: the man would hear very little of what we said because he was nearly stone deaf!

One by one we approached this wonderful old soul and spoke our good wishes and presented our gifts. When it came my turn, he kept looking up at me as I spoke and when he saw that my lips had stopped moving, he kept looking and said "YOU'RE GOING TO GIVE ME A SHAVE?"

AS THE CROW WALKS

A Newfoundlander was travelling on the mainland and became stranded on the highway. He flagged down a car and asked the driver, "How far is it to the next town butty?" The reply, "Nigh onto five miles as the crow flies."

Then the Newfoundlander asked, "But what if the crow has to walk and carry a gasoline can?"

ANOTHER TALL TALE

A fellow from the mainland was spending a vacation in one of our outports in the fall of the year.

He was quite impressed with the hunting abilities of one of the residents there. Every day this man was returning with a brace or two of rabbits. Others in the community did not do as well as that.

One day the visiting mainlander asked him, "How do you manage to do so well with the rabbits all the time?" The hunter replied, "Well b'y, I find me a rabbit track runnin' long be a rock an' I t'row a 'an'full a pepper on d'rock, an' as d'rabbits cross dey sneeze sa hard dey bates der brains out on d'rock."

H'ANGLICANS ARE HONEST?

About five years ago I was making regular visits to St. Luke's Anglican Home. One morning when making a call there to see my friend, it was raining quite hard and I used my umbrella from the parking lot to the home. I left the umbrella in the vestibule.

An hour later, when my visit was over I proceeded to the vestibule to pick up my umbrella but to my surprise as we say here in Newfoundland,

"There it was gone."

Well I said to myself, "Who's that so-and-so H'Anglican who took my umbrella?"

That afternoon I went downtown and bought a new umbrella. Two days later I returned to St. Luke's and there was my original umbrella back in the corner where I had left it. Well, did ya ever?

Telling an Anglican Reverend about this incident he asked me how did I know it was an Anglican who took the umbrella. I replied, "Because if it was anyone other than an Anglican he would probably have kept it." Which pleased him very much.

DO IT YOURSELF

A middle aged man was shuffling along bent over to the waist as his wife helped him into the doctors office.

The doctors attendant enquired sympathetically, "Arthritis with complications?"

To which the wife replied NO DO IT YOURSELF WITH CONCRETE BLOCKS.

HORSE-MOOSE MEAT

I was told about a fellow who kept a horse for hauling out wood wintertime. One day while in the woods the horse broke a leg and had to be shot. The owner had a friend with a mink ranch and he knew the mink rancher would be glad to have the horse to be fed to the mink. So the horse was butchered and the quarters hung from some trees in the woods. They were left there and the next day were to be carted to the ranch.

Two other guys who had also been in the woods came across the hung quarters of the horse. Thinking it was moose they stole a quarter.

They thought they had the luck of Riley until a few days later they heard about the fate of the horse and where the accident had happened. They knew right away it was horse meat they had and not moose.

When one fellow heard about it he had enjoyed two meals of the horse-moose meat that very day. Since a roast of horse was not his particular choice of meat he immediately became violently ill. Clutching his stomach he stumbled to a neighbour's house, who owned a horse-and-cart, to drive to the doctor's house. He said to the neighbour, "Take me to the doctor but for d'luv va God don't let me see d'horse."

A group of Newfoundland army recruits stood at attention, as their drill sargeant shouted: "My name is Stone, and I'm harder than my name. Get that straight right now, because this is going to be the toughest three months of your life."

Then he went from soldier to soldier, asking each one his name. When he reached the smallest recruit there was no response. "Are you ignoring me soldier?" he said, "I asked your name." In a hoarse whisper the young man replied: "Stone-breaker, sir!"

Two Newfoundland cargo vessels, one carrying a shipment of red paint, the other a shipment of blue collided at sea. There was no loss of life, but the crew ended up marooned.

TOO FISHY TO H'EAT

One night we had all told what our fathers did for a living and we added something to our story to give our listeners a laugh. Everyone had told something about he's father all except one. So someone turned to Jake and said, "Come on Jake b'y, cartny yer fauder 'ad to work fer a livin' didn't eh?" So Jake replied, "me fauder was a fisherman all his life. Did nuttin' but fish an' d'ya know b'ys when he died eh wuz too fishy to h'eat, we 'ad to bury'm."

TWO DEVILS

Pat owned a horse and carriage and often the Priest called upon Pat to drive him when on a visitation of the parish. The priest and the Methodist minister were good friends. One day seeing the minister on the road and going in the same direction he asked Pat to stop and give him a lift, which he did.

They were doing alright on the level but when they came to a steep hill the horse stopped and couldn't be coaxed to go.

Priest: Pat the other day you told me this horse could haul the devil.

Pat: Yes Fauder dat's true but not two devils.

WORTHWHILE OPINION

A henpecked Newfoundland husband was silent, as he watched his wife prepare to mount a very large picture of her mother on the living room wall.

"I simply can't decide the best place to put this picture of mother," she said, "I don't suppose you have a worthwhile opinion?"

"Well, I think hanging is too good for her," he replied.

INSPECTING COWS

A Federal Department of Agriculture agent was inspecting cows in the Codroy Valley area. He walked into the farmer's barnyard, flashed his identification and walked towards the cows, despite the farmer's yelling to stay behind the fence.

Just then a huge bull charged towards him, and the terrified agent shouted to the farmer to call him off.

"Show him your I.D." retorted the farmer, "he doesn't know who you are."

BLACKER THAN BLACK

About fifty years ago a Newfoundlander from one of the bays got a job on a vessel going to the Bahamas. As they docked they were informed that they'd be there for three weeks.

Now the Newfoundlander knew that the sun was supposed to be very strong and very hot down there in the Bahamas.

Later in the day, he came on deck and came face to face with the blackest man he had ever seen in his life. Since he had never seen a Negro before, he stared in amazement and then asked, "how long have you been here?" "Two days," was the reply. Then he blurted out, "how black am I gonna be when I'm here fer three weeks."

AILING BACKS

Ailing backs seem to be very popular in these modern times. However, people had bad backs years ago also, but they had homemade cures which seemed to work wonders.

A friend was telling me about a man whom he knew in the outports who had a very sore back. He had tried a lot of stuff but nuttin' worked, till finally a woman from up d'shore gave him a stick of Dragon's Blood, a dark red plaster used in early days. My friend said she did not know what it was herself but said her father used to use it along with a white stick plaster called diaculum.

You'd melt it and spread it on a piece of cloth for a plaster and wrapped it around the sore parts.

So the lady from up the shore gave the Dragon's Blood to Azariah and it did him so good that he wanted all the neighbours to know about it.

He was telling a group of them about it but couldn't rightly mind what it was called. He was deep in thought when a divil-skin-kind of fella come out with "Perhaps it was Sealing Wax?" Azariah got all excited and blurted out, "Yas b'y, yas b'y, dat's what t'were sailin' wax."

DOUGHB'YS

Abraham was one of these fellows who was always in church each Sunday. He often got hungry during the long drawn out sermons of the minister. He, as well as many others, also got bored. He could contend with the boredom but the hunger was something else. So he often took a lunch along.

This particular Sunday Abraham put four or five doughboys in a bag and stuffed them in his vest. That Sunday the minister read from the Old Testament and read his text, "Abraham, what hast thou in thy bosom?" Our friend came to life quickly and yelled at the Reverend, "doughb'ys, b'y, doughb'ys," and then flug one at him.

WAKE UP AND YER FIRED

A railway section foreman was walking along the line and he found two of his men sound asleep.

"Slape on, slape on ye lazy t'ings," he said with a smile. "as long as yer aslape yees got a job but soon as yees wake up yer fired."

CUTACUER H'OINTMENT

Before the days of public health Dr. Chase's patent medicines, Dodd's Kidney Pills, Cuticura Ointment, Mentholatum and such, all enjoyed quite a reputation and many were the claims made by their users regarding their miraculous healing powers.

I remember H'Uncle H'Andrew from Green's Pond who built my home. I met him one day and he was just recovering from a bout of shingles. He was much better when I met him but the shingles had left a very sore area under his arm that refused to heal. The doctor had prescribed a number of different h'ointments but none did a bit of good. He continued and told me that while suffering from the misery of the sore h'arm pit, he met a feller from 'ome, Greenspond. He heard H'Uncle H'Andrew's sad story and then he said, "H'Uncle H'Andrew, did youse try d'Cutacurer h'ointment?"

H'Uncle H'Andrew visited the drug store that afternoon and bought the Cutacuer h'Ointment. Eh smeared en on for mose a fartnight and eh 'ad a sore h'arm pit no more.

WEST VS D' NORDEAST

An old fellow and his son were both relaxing in Doucett's tavern. On returning from the bar with their drinks the father realized his son was being harassed by a mean bullying fellow.

The son was a quiet sort of guy and was trying to turn the other cheek in hopes the trouble would go away. But the old man was having none of it.

Placing the drinks on the table he grabbed buddy's arm, squinted an eye at him sideways and said for him to leave their table right now.

The mean fellow was known to be a rough guy and looking for trouble so he said, "lookut here, don't ya know I'm a 'Gale' from out west?" To which the old man roared, "I don't care if yer a hurricane from d' Nordeast."

BUNK OUT WITH STRANGERS

The lady said this story is true and it is believable for sure.

Five years ago my husband had a summer job at Churchill Falls. I decided I would visit with him for a few days. On the plane I sat near a lady who was also heading for Churchill Falls. Her husband had a summer job too.

Just before we were to land at Churchill Falls an announcement came over the P.A. that it was too foggy to land and we would land at Goose Bay for overnight.

We were taken to the Goose Hotel, there was thirteen of us. The clerk of the hotel informed us that there was a shortage of rooms, and she asked if some of us would "double up". I readily agreed that I would share a room with my new found friend.

The room to which we were assigned had only one double bed. As we got ready to "bunk it out", I started to laugh. My friend looked bewildered and said, "what's so funny?" I replied, "y'know when I was a girl my mother told me not to get in cars with strangers . . . she should see me now . . . I'm getting in bed with one."

A SUBSTITUTE FOR PROBABTION

This story comes from the court in Corner Brook.

A fourteen old boy was up before court for drinking under age. He was guilty and the Judge told him he was putting him on probation. The Judge told him what probation was all about and then asked him where he had gotten the liquor. He then pointed to his father who was in the court and said his father had given it to him.

The Judge then talked to the father and asked him if he had liquor in the home would he dispose of it right away. The father refused absolutely. The Judge then told him it would be useless to have his son put on probation if he was to be exposed to liquor in his home.

The court room was in an uproar for a minute after that because the father raised his voice and said,

"OK, YER HONOUR, OW'S ABOUT DIS. D'NEX' TOIME OI WANTS A DRINK, OI KICK ME ZON OUTA DOORS. DAT SOUNDS GOOD ENOUGH DOESN'T UT?"

GRACE

There was nine boys in our family. When I received the following story I was reminded how it was at our home when the dinner was on the table and grace was ready to be said. My dad would say, "BEHAVE, BEHAVE", and we did.

A lady was saying grace and her children were behaving badly. She had to stop and bawl at them in between her words. Her grace went something like this—

Lord have mercy on our souls
DON'T YOU DARE TASTE THEM ROLLS
and the food we're going to eat
YOU KEEP STILL I SEES THY FEET
DON'T YOU TRY THAT TRICK AGAIN
Give us joy and peace.
AMEN!

THE BISHOP

The bishop sent a letter to the vicar advising him that he would be visiting on the last Sunday of the month.

The particular Sunday rolled around and when the Bishop and Vicar entered the church there were only three people in the sanctuary.

Bishop: Did you let it be known that I was coming?

Vicar: No, but it seems the word got around.

HELL OR HEAVEN

We have all heard stories of people who cannot resist the temptation to fall asleep in church. Some are regular church sleepers and today's story is about a regular.

This fellow had it right down to a science as we say. Each Sunday the minister had not gotten into the sermon too far before he would be asleep, but somehow he would manage to wake just at the tail end of the sermon.

This particular Sunday the preacher was on the subject of Heaven and Hell. He became very enthusiastic close to the end of the sermon and said, "All those who want to go to Heaven stand up!" Of course all those in the body of the church stood up, all except our sleeper.

The preacher's next announcement was, "all those who want to go to Hell stand up!" Our sleeper had just become conscious and heard only the last two words 'stand up'. He came to his feet immediately. But seeing he was the only member of the congregation and the minister were standing, he said to the minister, "well, Reverend what ever we are voting for it seems that there are only two of us for it."

LAUGHTER

Morally considered, laughter is next to the Ten Commandments, and according to medical reports, laughter *stimulates* the *vasomotor centers*, and the epasmodic contraction of the blood vessels causing the blood to flow quickly.

Laughter too, accelerates the respiration and gives warmth and glow to the whole system. It brightens the eye, increases the respiration, expands the chest, forces the air from the least used cells and tends to restore the exquisite poise and balance that we call health.

All this and Heaven too, laughter may also serve to restore one's hearing. It is actually one of the best types of physical exercise; and it is available to many to whom no other *exercise* is practical.

(Found in a medical book)